The 5–
Minute
BIBLE
STUDY
for Men

Jess MacCallum

The 5–Minute BIBLE STUDY for Men

Seeking God's Wisdom

BARBOUR
PUBLISHING

INTRODUCTION

Do you find it hard to make time for Bible study? You intend to do it, but with your daily demands and distractions, it just seems to get crowded out. And where do you start anyway? With a specific book or chapter? With a topic or question?

This book provides a simple way for you to begin to develop the habit of daily, personal Bible study—even if you only have five minutes. It's a small but intentional investment of your time that will see great returns in your life.

First, let's look at how it works:

- Minutes 1–2: *Read* carefully the scripture passage for each day's Bible study.

- Minute 3: *Contemplate* a few questions designed to help you unpack these verses and dig deeper into what the author was trying to communicate.

- Minute 4: *Apply.* Read a reflection based on the day's scriptural focus. Think about what you are learning and how to apply these truths to your own life.

- Minute 5: *Pray.* A prayer starter will help you to begin a time of conversation with God. Remember to allow time for Him to speak into your life as well.

Second, the process above could apply to any passage or topic in the Bible. For this book, we've chosen the *wisdom of God*. As you'll see, wisdom is part of the deepest mysteries of God but also the simplest tasks of daily life; wisdom was God's companion at the beginning and our companion today. We'll look at wisdom's counterpart—foolishness—and study stories and parables that demonstrate both.

Finally, while the Bible speaks to all people, this book is aimed at men's particular journey. Of course, men are not all identical, but we do share many common traits and challenges. If there are elements of this book that you don't feel fit you or your stage in life, simply let the Word of God speak for itself in your unique situation. Sometimes what you learn in Bible study today will come back to you in the future as the Spirit uses His words in His time.

May *The 5-Minute Bible Study for Men* help you to establish the habit of studying God's Word. Your willingness to spend these minutes focused on God's Word and prayer can make a huge difference in your day, in your life, and in the lives of those around you!

BEFORE THE BEGINNING

Read Proverbs 8:22–31

Key Verses:

The Lord possessed me at the beginning of his work,
the first of his acts of old. Ages ago I was set up,
at the first, before the beginning of the earth.
Proverbs 8:22–23 esv

Contemplate:

- Did wisdom exist before creation?
- Why do you think wisdom speaks as if it were a person?

Apply:

Well beyond the first chapter of Genesis, God as Creator is referenced over and over, emphasizing His authority and supremacy. Prophets, kings, and psalmists echo Jeremiah's words: "It is he who made the earth by his power, who established the world by his wisdom, and by his understanding stretched out the heavens" (Jeremiah 10:12 esv). There is no room for doubt that God is the supreme author of creation. But there are hints, as in today's passage, of another "person" involved in creation; wisdom, speaking as a person, declares "I was set up. . .before the beginning of the earth" which begs the question:

is this simply poetic language or was someone else involved in creation?

The apostle John reveals this profound mystery: "In the beginning was the Word, and the Word *was with* God, and the Word *was* God. He was in the beginning with God. All things were made through him, and without him was not any thing made that was made" (John 1:1–3 ESV). As wisdom speaks in Proverbs 8, we gain insight into the thoughts and emotions of Jesus as He and His Father created the world: "when he [God] marked out the foundations of the earth, then I [wisdom/Word] was beside him, like a master workman, and I was daily his delight, rejoicing before him always, rejoicing in his inhabited world and delighting in the children of man" (Proverbs 8:29–31 ESV).

PRAY:

Creator God, thank You for making a world
that You delighted in and shared with us.
I rejoice in being re-created in Christ and
being a delight to You once again!

WISDOM HIMSELF

Read 1 Corinthians 1:26–31

KEY VERSE:

God has united you with Christ Jesus. For our benefit God made him to be wisdom itself. Christ made us right with God; he made us pure and holy, and he freed us from sin.

1 CORINTHIANS 1:30 NLT

CONTEMPLATE:

- What does it mean to be "united" with Christ?
- Who is the very essence of wisdom?
- What does it mean to be "made right" with God?

APPLY:

To really apply the wisdom of God in our lives, we need to grasp that Jesus Christ is wisdom embodied. He is its origin and its essence; He is its source and its goal. For us to understand any verse in the Bible about wisdom—from its role in the creation to Solomon's very specific instructions to Paul's discourse in 1 Corinthians on human philosophy—we must understand this most foundational truth.

Jesus made this dramatic claim about Himself: "I am the way, the truth, and the life. No one can come to the Father except through me" (John 14:6 NLT). He wasn't saying He could show us the way to the Father or that He knew the truth about God or was the path to new life but that He was the living definition of those things. It's the same with wisdom. In other words, to speak of wisdom without Jesus Christ is to speak of something man made, something limited and incomplete. Wisdom apart from Him is—at best—calling a shadow a real person.

In this book, we'll be looking at many aspects and examples of the wisdom of God. And they will all harken back to this most central fact: Jesus is our wisdom, and nothing will make sense apart from Him.

PRAY:

Father, you've united us with Your Son and given us life! And in Him, we find living wisdom! Thank You. Lead us to become more like Jesus, walking daily in His wisdom.

BUILDING A FIRM
FOUNDATION

Read Psalm 111

KEY VERSE:

The fear of the LORD is the beginning of wisdom;
all those who follow His commandments have a
good understanding; His praise endures forever.
PSALM 111:10 NASB

CONTEMPLATE:

- What is the meaning of "fear" in this context?

- Why is this kind of fear necessary for wisdom?

- What promises are made to the one who obeys?

APPLY:

To continue building on a firm biblical foundation and truly grasp the wisdom of God and how it applies to our lives, we have to consider what some may think of as an odd component. The psalmist declares that "the fear of the Lord"—the awe, wonder, and respect of the Creator of all things—is our starting point for a proper understanding. The fear of the Lord is not the same as being scared of Him, though He can and should be terrifying to those who embrace wickedness and love sin. For His children, fearing their Father-King is the beginning of seeing His creation as it really is, His authority as it really is, and our lives in this world as they really are.

Once we begin exercising the proper perspective by applying the fear of the Lord to our daily lives, we start seeing things differently. That's where we begin to grow in wisdom, but there's more. Throughout the Bible, wisdom is not merely insight or an intellectual experience. It's bound together with right actions and right living. As today's Key Verse points out, "those who follow His commandments" are the ones who gain understanding. It's similar to playing a sport or musical instrument: you gain understanding as you practice.

PRAY:

Lord, God of all creation, bless me with a heart that fears You in holiness and reverence that I may gain wisdom. And help me to obey Your commandments that I may grow in my understanding of You.

THE HOME OF WISDOM

Read Psalm 51

KEY VERSE:

*Behold, You desire truth in the innermost being,
and in secret You will make wisdom known to me.*
PSALM 51:6 NASB

CONTEMPLATE:

- What does God desire that we possess?
- How does God choose to reveal wisdom to us?

APPLY:

One of the recurring themes in the Bible is the importance of our "innermost being." Sometimes words like *heart, soul,* or *mind* are used to describe this inner part of us. When Moses commanded the people to love the Lord "with all your heart and with all your soul and with all your strength" (Deuteronomy 6:5 NIV), he wasn't describing individual parts but rather emphasizing that the whole inner man is to be involved.

Our innermost being is the source of our thoughts and our values, thus making it the seat of our choices and actions. In Psalm 51, David confessed his outward sin of adultery with Bathsheba but knew his failing originated from within and cried out, "Create in me a pure *heart*, O God, and renew a steadfast spirit within me" (Psalm 51:10 NIV). If the inner man changes, the outer man must follow.

In Christ, we experience even more than David asked for. Jesus said that if anyone loved and obeyed Him, He *and* the Father would "come to him and make our home with him" (John 14:23 ESV) through the Holy Spirit. That inner fact, Jesus claimed, produces an outward effect: "The one who believes in Me, as the Scripture said, 'From his innermost being will flow rivers of living water'" (John 7:38 NASB).

Jesus *is* truth and wisdom, and as He lives in us, our lives *will* reflect His presence. "Whoever says 'I know him' but does not keep his commandments is a liar, and the truth is not in him" (1 John 2:4 ESV).

PRAY:

Author of all truth, help me to listen to Your voice in the secret place where You give me life.

WISDOM'S PURPOSE

Read Ephesians 1:15–22

KEY VERSES:

For this reason, ever since I heard about your faith in the Lord Jesus and your love for all God's people, I have not stopped giving thanks for you, remembering you in my prayers. I keep asking that the God of our Lord Jesus Christ, the glorious Father, may give you the Spirit of wisdom and revelation, so that you may know him better.

EPHESIANS 1:15–17 NIV

CONTEMPLATE:

- What kind of believers was Paul addressing?

- What was Paul's response to the testimony of the Ephesians?

- What did he ask God for and why?

APPLY:

As we study the Word, we'll employ various Bible study techniques, one of which is to simply compare different translations. Good translations attempt a *word-for-word* rendering. However, there are many occasions when scholars must use a *meaning-for-meaning* approach. For example, in today's reading, the phrase "give you the Spirit of wisdom" can also be expressed "give you a spirit of wisdom" (NASB), or "give you spiritual wisdom" (NLT). These options help clarify that Paul wasn't asking for the Holy Spirit to come again to these believers but for something very specific—a unique kind of wisdom and insight. And for a specific purpose.

For God's children, there's nothing better than to grow up in faith and mature in Christ. That growth, Paul prayed, would encompass three things: "I pray that the eyes of your heart may be enlightened in order that you may know the hope to which he has called you, the riches of his glorious inheritance in his holy people, and his incomparably great power for us who believe" (Ephesians 1:18–19 NIV). These three things were on Paul's heart for all believers. He prayed constantly for them to *know*, not just *believe*. Next, we'll see why Paul considered these so important for us.

PRAY:

Glorious Father, I want to receive the wisdom Paul prayed for so earnestly and know You more!

WISDOM'S PURPOSE: HOPE

Read Ephesians 1:15–22

KEY VERSES:

Having the eyes of your hearts enlightened, that you may know what is the hope to which he has called you, what are the riches of his glorious inheritance in the saints, and what is the immeasurable greatness of his power toward us who believe, according to the working of his great might.
EPHESIANS 1:18–19 ESV

CONTEMPLATE:

- How is spiritual hope different from worldly hope?

- Where does the hope of a believer come from?

APPLY:

Certain elements will be repeated as we study wisdom since they're tied closely to the subject. As we've seen, *heart, soul,* and *mind* are all used to describe our innermost being. While often interchangeable, the nuances of language can add special emphasis. Paul's phrase "eyes of the heart" points us to the center and deepest part of our being. This is where the "spirit of wisdom and revelation" begins to move us beyond believing to knowing the truth in our hearts, starting with our hope in Christ.

The hope we are called to is, simply put, eternal life. Certainly, we experience hope in Christ in daily life, for "If we have hoped in Christ *only in this life*, we are of all people most to be pitied. But the fact is, Christ has been raised from the dead" (1 Corinthians 15:19-20 NASB). Paul was looking ahead "with eager hope for the day when God will give us our full rights as his adopted children, including the new bodies he has promised us. We were given this hope when we were saved" (Romans 8:23–24 NLT).

Peter also emphasized that God "caused us to be born again to a living hope through the resurrection of Jesus Christ from the dead" (1 Peter 1:3 NASB). Our hope of eternal life only exists because of the fact of His resurrection.

PRAY:

God of hope, may I know and live out the truth of the eternal life You've promised.

WISDOM'S PURPOSE: INHERITANCE

Read Ephesians 1:15–22

KEY VERSES:

I pray that the eyes of your heart may be enlightened in order that you may know the hope to which he has called you, the riches of his glorious inheritance in his holy people and his incomparably great power for us who believe.
EPHESIANS 1:18–19 NIV

CONTEMPLATE:

- What kind of inheritance is Paul talking about?

- Who gets this inheritance?

APPLY:

Part of the covenant with Abraham included the promise of a homeland that would pass down to future generations. "And I will give to you and to your offspring after you the land of your sojournings, all the land of Canaan" (Genesis 17:8 ESV). Though the patriarchs occupied some areas of Canaan, it took more than four centuries for Israel to begin settling the Promised Land. Therefore, being new to land ownership, Moses provided laws concerning its use and how it would pass to the next generation.

The Hebrew root for "inheritance" (*nachal*), means "stream" or "river," so an inheritance was a blessing flowing to the recipients. We have every reason to get excited about our eternal blessing in Christ—"an inheritance that is imperishable, undefiled, and unfading, kept in heaven for you" (1 Peter 1:4 esv). But we're not the only ones looking forward to that day!

God is eager for "his glorious inheritance in his holy people." God created Israel "the people of [His] inheritance, whom [He] redeemed" (Psalm 74:2 niv) from Abraham to be His own. David sang, "Blessed is the nation whose God is the Lord, the people he chose for his inheritance" (Psalm 33:12 niv). Through the faith-based covenant begun with Abraham and fulfilled in Christ, the Father sought "to purify for Himself a people for His own possession" (Titus 2:14 nasb). Imagine. . .God is excited about what He's going to get one day in us!

Pray:

*Lord, I am humbled to be Your own possession.
Help me to live that truth every day.*

WISDOM'S PURPOSE: POWER

Read Ephesians 1:15–22

KEY VERSES:

I pray that the eyes of your heart may be enlightened, so that you will know what is the hope of His calling, what are the riches of the glory of His inheritance in the saints, and what is the boundless greatness of His power toward us who believe.

EPHESIANS 1:18–19 NASB

CONTEMPLATE:

- What characterizes God's power?
- Who benefits from this power?

APPLY:

Our final day with this passage shows just how much can be packed into a few lines of scripture! St. Jerome, the scholar behind the Latin *Vulgate* (the Bible of Western Europe for a thousand years), captured this feeling well: "The scriptures are shallow enough for a babe to come and drink without fear of drowning and deep enough for theologians to swim in without ever touching the bottom."

Comparing translations as we have before, we find "the boundless greatness of His power," also rendered, "incomparably great power" (NIV) and "immeasurable greatness" (ESV). The Amplified Bible, which attempts to express the fullest meaning of each phrase, says: "the immeasurable and unlimited and surpassing greatness." In any reading, it's big!

Paul goes on to explain how this power benefits us: "This is the same mighty power that raised Christ from the dead and seated him in the place of honor at God's right hand in the heavenly realms" (Ephesians 1:19–20 NLT) where we will join Him one day. Everything we hope for in Christ, and everything God hopes for in us, rests on the Risen Messiah.

With Paul, we should pray for the gift of the "spirit of wisdom and revelation" (Ephesians 1:17 ESV) to know God more, and believe His word, thus avoiding the rebuke of the skeptics of the resurrection: "You are mistaken, since you do not understand the Scriptures nor the power of God" (Matthew 22:29 NASB).

PRAY:

Open the eyes of my heart, O Lord,
to embrace all that You have promised.

THE END AND THE MEANS

Read Genesis 3

KEY VERSE:

The woman was convinced. She saw that the tree was beautiful and its fruit looked delicious, and she wanted the wisdom it would give her. So she took some of the fruit and ate it. Then she gave some to her husband, who was with her, and he ate it, too.

GENESIS 3:6 NLT

CONTEMPLATE:

- Where was the man when the woman was having a conversation with the serpent?
- What about the fruit appealed to the woman?

APPLY:

In the garden of Eden, everything was good. The woman was not wrong for desiring wisdom. But there were some serious problems with the way she pursued it. Before we lay all the blame on the woman, though, let's look at the whole story.

In Genesis 2:15–17, when God commanded the man not to eat of that *one* tree, he was alone; the command came prior to the woman's existence—so how did she know about it? From her husband. It was his responsibility to instruct her. When the serpent asked her, "Did God really say. . ." (Genesis 3:1 NIV), he was questioning her trust in her husband just as much as in God's command. And apparently, the man added to God's prohibition since the woman includes, "and you must not touch it" (Genesis 3:3 NIV) in her reply to the serpent's question. That may have been a wise addition, but nonetheless, in the critical moment, the man "who was with her" (verse 6) didn't step up. He sided with his wife's reasoning over God's command (Genesis 3:17).

They both missed something essential: true wisdom can't exist apart from simple obedience. No amount of rationalizing, even well intentioned, can substitute for that. Whether we use our rational gifts to obey or justify our own path is the real test of wisdom.

PRAY:

*Lord God, protect me from my own
imagination when it tries to compete with
Your clear and loving commands!*

YEARS DO NOT
ALWAYS MATTER

Read Job 32

KEY VERSES:

*Now Elihu had waited before speaking to Job
because they were older than he. . . . "I am young
in years, and you are old; that is why I was fearful,
not daring to tell you what I know. I thought,
'Age should speak; advanced years should teach
wisdom.' But it is the spirit in a person, the breath
of the Almighty, that gives them understanding.
It is not only the old who are wise, not only
the aged who understand what is right."*

JOB 32:4–9 NIV

CONTEMPLATE:

- Is there a relationship between age and
  wisdom?

- Where does wisdom come from?

APPLY:

Job famously experienced tremendous suffering as
part of God's eternal and often mysterious plan.
One thing is clear from the first chapter: Job was not
being punished for any sin. But three close friends

still tried to persuade him that his predicament was somehow his fault. Their counsel was based on worldly arguments and theological assumptions that missed the mark. Then a younger man named Elihu appears, taking Job to task "for justifying himself rather than God" (Job 32:2 NIV). Job's situation was not caused by his sin, but it did lead him to demand the Almighty explain Himself to a man.

Elihu was slow to join the conversation out of respect for his elders. But seeing that they lacked real insight, he spoke up to correct their error. Elihu demonstrated that age doesn't guarantee wisdom. The only source of wisdom is "the breath of the Almighty" (Job 32:8 NIV). Paul echoes this belief in his advice to Timothy: "Don't let anyone look down on you because you are young, but set an example for the believers in speech, in conduct, in love, in faith and in purity" (1 Timothy 4:12 NIV).

PRAY:

Breath of Life, fill me with wisdom through Your Holy Spirit. Teach me when to listen to others and when to speak words of sound counsel.

Asking for Wisdom

Read James 1:1–7

Key Verses:

*If any of you lacks wisdom, you should ask God,
who gives generously to all without finding fault,
and it will be given to you. But when you ask,
you must believe and not doubt, because the one
who doubts is like a wave of the sea, blown and
tossed by the wind. That person should not expect
to receive anything from the Lord. Such a person
is double-minded and unstable in all they do.*

James 1:5–8 niv

Contemplate:

- Can anyone ask for wisdom?

- How are we to approach God when seeking wisdom?

- How does God respond to those who seek Him?

Apply:

For those of us who feel a deficit of wisdom, it's encouraging to hear James say God gives it generously. . . even if there's a small catch.

God is a generous Father to His children. In fact, He's so generous by nature that He even provides for those who ignore Him. When Jesus commanded His disciples to love their enemies, He tied it directly to acting like their Father in heaven who "causes His sun to rise on the evil and the good, and sends rain on the righteous and the unrighteous" (Matthew 5:45 NASB).

As sons, we have a unique relationship with our gracious Father, and thus we never face conditional love; we don't have every shortcoming pointed out before receiving His blessing. But we do face one condition when asking for wisdom: we must believe. Our doubt creates an obstacle even for our generous Father. In fact, belief is fundamental to receiving any of God's gifts, starting with salvation. "If you declare with your mouth, 'Jesus is Lord,' and believe in your heart that God raised him from the dead, you will be saved" (Romans 10:9 NIV). James says a "double-minded" man shouldn't expect to receive anything from the Lord.

PRAY:
Gracious Father, I happily accept the wisdom You want me to have!

WISDOM FROM ABOVE

Read James 3

KEY VERSES:

Who is wise and understanding among you? Let them show it by their good life, by deeds done in the humility that comes from wisdom. But if you harbor bitter envy and selfish ambition in your hearts, do not boast about it or deny the truth. Such "wisdom" does not come down from heaven but is earthly, unspiritual, demonic. For where you have envy and selfish ambition, there you find disorder and every evil practice.

JAMES 3:13–16 NIV

CONTEMPLATE:

- How is wisdom recognized?
- What characterizes wisdom that is not from heaven?
- What is the root of "earthly" wisdom?

APPLY:

As we've seen from earlier studies, wisdom from God is a way of life. In the books of the Bible known as "wisdom literature" are recorded helpful, practical advice. Those books are always concerned about us living wisely before God and man. James, whose entire letter is about actions speaking louder than words, echoes their sentiment.

What we really believe and cherish comes out in our lives for all to witness. This is the principle Jesus described when rebuking the Pharisees: "A good man brings good things out of the good stored up in him, and an evil man brings evil things out of the evil stored up in him" (Matthew 12:35 NIV). Whether we "harbor bitter envy and selfish ambition" in our hearts, or desire to honor the Lord, the evidence is found in our day-to-day walk. For people in love with this world, an "earthly, unspiritual, demonic" approach to life passes for a type of wisdom. Some write best-selling business books while others just brag to their friends. But as children of the Almighty, we are to reflect something grander—the "wisdom from above" (James 3:17 ESV).

PRAY:

Father, fill my heart and mind with Your
Word and lead me to live according to
the humility of heavenly wisdom.

WISDOM IS. . .PURE

Read James 3:13–18

KEY VERSE:

*But the wisdom from above is first pure,
then peaceable, gentle, open to reason, full of
mercy and good fruits, impartial and sincere.*
JAMES 3:17 ESV

CONTEMPLATE:

- What does "pure" mean in this context?
- Why would James list it first here?

APPLY:

Bible study begins with simple observations. That means trying to discover what a passage would have meant to the original reader rather than making assumptions or introducing a modern, or even theological, bias. Sound observations make interpretation and application much easier.

Basic observations include knowing who's speaking, who the audience is, and what cultural and political situations might be in play. It also includes defining words to the best of our ability both in English and in the original Hebrew or Greek. And with today's online resources, there's no easier time in history to dig deeper!

The Greek word translated as "pure" is *hagnē* which includes the concepts of undivided or clean, much in the same way English would describe gold or silver being uncontaminated by other elements. But there's one other interesting meaning to this word found in *Thayer's Greek Lexicon*—"exciting reverence." The wisdom from above is not only completely uncontaminated; it causes reverence and awe. It's motivating because of its purity.

We've all seen old westerns where the grizzled prospector works his claim on some lonely mountain, then takes his find to the assayer in town to test it. The question wasn't, did he find gold, but how *pure* was the gold? The less contaminated, the more exciting his find. Likewise, since Jesus Himself is our wisdom from above, we can have utter confidence that His commands are uncontaminated and trustworthy.

In the next few studies, we'll see how each of the characteristics James uses to describe wisdom is embodied in Christ.

PRAY:

*Lord God, thank You for the purity of
Your commands and how trustworthy
every word You say is!*

WISDOM IS. . .PEACEABLE

Read James 3:13–18

KEY VERSE:

But the wisdom from above is first pure, then
peaceable, gentle, open to reason, full of mercy
and good fruits, impartial and sincere.

JAMES 3:17 ESV

CONTEMPLATE:

- What does "peaceable" mean in this context?

- How would a peaceable person behave?

- How does seeking peace demonstrate wisdom?

APPLY:

To continue our observations in James 3:17, let's look at the Greek word for *peaceable (eirēnikē)* sometimes translated as "peace-loving." Either of those work well in English, but the root word also implies an additional idea beyond simply avoiding strife or conflict—reconciliation.

Reconciliation was at the very heart of Jesus' purpose for coming into the world. The gospel itself is "the good news of peace through Jesus Christ" (Acts 10:36 NIV). And not just between man and God, but between Jew and Gentile:

"For [Jesus] himself is our peace, who has made the two groups one and has destroyed the barrier, the dividing wall of hostility, by setting aside in his flesh the law with its commands and regulations. His purpose was to create in himself one new humanity out of the two, thus making peace, and in one body to reconcile both of them to God through the cross, by which he put to death their hostility. He came and preached peace to you who were far away and peace to those who were near. For through him we both have access to the Father by one Spirit." (Ephesians 2:14–18 NIV)

In the miraculous solution of the cross, God offered salvation to those under the Law *and* to those outside the covenant equally since both needed Jesus. "But to those called by God to salvation, both Jews and Gentiles, Christ is the power of God and the wisdom of God" (1 Corinthians 1:24 NLT). The wisdom from above seeks the peace of reconciliation.

PRAY:

Father, how awesome is the reconciliation You planned for us in Your Son at the cross!

WISDOM IS. . .GENTLE

Read James 3:13–18

KEY VERSE:

But the wisdom from above is first pure, then peaceable, gentle, open to reason, full of mercy and good fruits, impartial and sincere.

JAMES 3:17 ESV

CONTEMPLATE:

- What does "gentle" mean in this context?
- How would a gentle person behave?
- How does seeking to be gentle demonstrate wisdom?

APPLY:

This passage is so rich that we need to park on it for a while! It will help lay the foundation for later studies as we look at the Proverbs and other wisdom literature and as we follow one of the most important rules of Bible study: allowing scripture to interpret scripture. By using one passage as a tool to understand another, we gain a fuller understanding and become "like the owner of a house who brings out of his storeroom new treasures as well as old" (Matthew 13:52 NIV).

This principle is demonstrated well in three passages about the gentle Messiah who was to come, rather than a conquering king. In the first, Jesus says, "Take My yoke upon you and learn from Me, for I am gentle and humble in heart, and YOU WILL FIND REST FOR YOUR SOULS" (Matthew 11:29 NASB). Jesus applies Jeremiah 6:16 to Himself, claiming to be the salvation Jeremiah rebuked Israel for rejecting.

Likewise, a gentle Messiah was promised by Isaiah: "Here is my servant whom I have chosen, the one I love, in whom I delight. . . . A bruised reed he will not break, and a smoldering wick he will not snuff out" (Matthew 12:17–20 NIV).

And when Jesus rode into Jerusalem He fulfilled Zechariah 9:9. "See, your king comes to you, gentle and riding on a donkey" (Matthew 21:5 NIV). In wisdom, God sent a gentle King to a hurting and lost world and spoke of it over and over through His prophets—though many did not see it.

PRAY:

Gentle Savior, You humbled Yourself to bring salvation and life. I give You thanks!

WISDOM IS. . .
OPEN TO REASON

Read James 3:13–18

KEY VERSE:

But the wisdom from above is first pure, then peaceable, gentle, open to reason, full of mercy and good fruits, impartial and sincere.
JAMES 3:17 ESV

CONTEMPLATE:

- What does being "open to reason" mean?

- How would a reasonable person speak to those who disagree with him?

APPLY:

A quick way to get a better understanding of a verse if you don't have time to research the Hebrew or Greek is by comparing various English translations. Some websites and apps will actually display multiple translations side by side to see how scholars render the meaning. Using this method, we see that "open to reason" can also be translated as "reasonable, willing to listen, approachable, sensible."

From the beginning, God has been more than willing to listen to and engage His people for their benefit. Just after Adam and Eve sinned, God approached them in the garden and asked four questions: "Where are you?" "Who told you that you were naked?" "Have you eaten of the tree. . .?" and "What is this that you have done?" (Genesis 3:9–13 ESV). It was not for His benefit that an omniscient Creator asked questions but for theirs.

Similarly, Jesus asked questions He already knew the answer to. "And behold, a lawyer stood up to put him to the test, saying, 'Teacher, what shall I do to inherit eternal life?' He said to him, 'What is written in the Law? How do you read it?'" (Luke 10:25–26 ESV). Jesus certainly didn't need a lesson in the Law! Likewise, Paul "reasoned in the synagogue with the Jews and the devout persons, and in the marketplace every day with those who happened to be there" (Acts 17:17 ESV).

Wisdom from above doesn't debate to win an argument, it reasons to open people's eyes.

PRAY:
Father in heaven, help me to listen to others and engage them with Your truth for their good.

WISDOM IS. . . FULL OF MERCY

Read James 3:13–18

KEY VERSE:

But the wisdom from above is first pure, then peaceable, gentle, open to reason, full of mercy and good fruits, impartial and sincere.

JAMES 3:17 ESV

CONTEMPLATE:

- Why does being full of something indicate good or bad?

- How is showing mercy wise?

- How have you experienced mercy from God?

APPLY:

This is the first of two traits to which James adds an interesting descriptor—"full of." This is the same term used to describe a net full of fish (John 21:8) or the Pharisees' hypocrisy (Matthew 23:28). There's no room for more.

Nothing characterizes divinity more than mercy. *Merriam-Webster* defines it as "compassion or forbearance shown especially to an offender or to one subject to one's power." What could better describe God's dealings with humankind from the beginning than mercy? Adam and Eve experienced it from the very moment they sinned, as God "made garments of skin for Adam and his wife, and clothed them" (Genesis 3:21 NASB). Despite mischaracterizations of the "God of the Old Testament" as harsh and judgmental, there are far more instances of His mercy. Noah, all the patriarchs, and Moses knew Him as "a God merciful and gracious, slow to anger, and abounding in steadfast love and faithfulness" (Exodus 34:6 ESV).

Jesus is the fulfillment of God's promise, as His mother Mary understood when she sang, "He has helped his servant Israel, in remembrance of his mercy, as he spoke to our fathers, to Abraham and to his offspring forever" (Luke 1:54–55 ESV). In Christ, we avoid the judgment we deserved, since, "According to his great mercy, he has caused us to be born again to a living hope through the resurrection of Jesus Christ from the dead" (1 Peter 1:3 ESV). As James declared: "Mercy triumphs over judgment" (James 2:13 NASB).

PRAY:

Merciful Father, compassionate Savior,
I thank You for the mystery of the cross
and the mercy found in Jesus.

WISDOM IS. . . FULL OF GOOD FRUITS

Read James 3:13–18

KEY VERSE:

But the wisdom from above is first pure, then peaceable, gentle, open to reason, full of mercy and good fruits, impartial and sincere.

JAMES 3:17 ESV

CONTEMPLATE:

- What does the figure of speech "good fruits" refer to?

- What is the relationship between wisdom and actions?

APPLY:

The figurative use of "fruits" in English is the same in the Greek—the results of one's choices and actions, whether good or bad. "A healthy tree cannot bear bad fruit, nor can a diseased tree bear good fruit" (Matthew 7:18 ESV). The tree determines the produce.

We begin to bear good fruit when we sink our roots deep into God: "Blessed is the man who trusts in the LORD, whose trust is the LORD. He is like a tree planted by water, that sends out its roots by the stream, and does not fear when heat comes, for its leaves remain green, and is not anxious in the year of drought, for it does not cease to bear fruit" (Jeremiah 17:7–8 ESV).

The Bible speaks of two kinds of fruit—inner and outer. Paul lists the inner fruit we bear when walking with Jesus: "The fruit of the Spirit is love, joy, peace, patience, kindness, goodness, faithfulness, gentleness, self-control" (Galatians 5:22–23 ESV). Likewise, walking in the wisdom from above leads also to outward fruit. Jesus told His disciples shortly before His crucifixion: "You did not choose Me but I chose you, and appointed you that you would go and bear fruit, and that your fruit would remain" (John 15:16 NASB). Their calling and assignment were to bring others into the kingdom.

Godly wisdom always leads to godly actions and to God's results.

PRAY:

Lord, You have given me a path that bears fruit inside and out; help me to trust in You for the strength to always walk in Christ's wisdom.

WISDOM IS. . .
IMPARTIAL AND SINCERE

Read James 3:13–18

KEY VERSE:

But the wisdom from above is first pure, then peaceable, gentle, open to reason, full of mercy and good fruits, impartial and sincere.
JAMES 3:17 ESV

CONTEMPLATE:

- How does an impartial person behave?

- How important is sincerity when we share our faith?

- What common elements do these two traits share?

APPLY:

Our last look at James 3:17 is a good opportunity to again compare other English translations for clarity. Many versions, such as the King James, phrase it negatively: "without partiality, and without hypocrisy." Remember that "wisdom from above is *first* pure." Without impartiality and sincerity, wisdom couldn't be pure—it would be suspect to contamination. In fact, if either of these traits were missing, then the other characteristics wouldn't matter because you could never trust this kind of wisdom.

Being impartial and sincere both have to do with trustworthiness. An impartial person shows no favoritism and treats people equally. James condemns favoritism, as when treating the rich better than the poor in the church: "Doesn't this discrimination show that your judgments are guided by evil motives?" (James 2:4 NLT). It may seem "wise" to treat big donors better than poorer members—but not in God's eyes!

Similarly, a sincere person can be trusted since he has no hidden agenda. You don't have to wonder what he really means. You can take him at his word. Paul elegantly connected wisdom, sincerity, and integrity in a single statement: "Now this is our boast: Our conscience testifies that we have conducted ourselves in the world, and especially in our relations with you, with integrity and godly sincerity. We have done so, relying not on worldly wisdom but on God's grace" (2 Corinthians 1:12 NIV).

Impartiality and sincerity are crucial to wisdom because they produce trust.

PRAY:

Heavenly Father, teach me to be honest, sincere, and fair in all my ways to honor You before all men.

GROWING WITH THE WORD, PART 1

Read 2 Timothy 3:10–17

KEY VERSE:

From childhood you have known the sacred writings which are able to give you the wisdom that leads to salvation through faith which is in Christ Jesus.
2 TIMOTHY 3:15 NASB

CONTEMPLATE:

- What are "the sacred writings" Paul refers to in today's Key Verse?

- What is the point of these sacred writings?

- When did Timothy begin learning from these sacred writings?

APPLY:

Today's focus comes from Paul's exhortation to his "beloved son" in the faith, Timothy (2 Timothy 1:2 NASB). Acts 16 records their meeting during Paul's second missionary journey in Asia Minor. Timothy, a believer with a Jewish mother but a Greek father, had a strong spiritual lineage: "For I am mindful of the sincere faith within you, which first dwelled in your grandmother Lois and your mother Eunice, and I am sure that it is in you as well" (2 Timothy 1:5 NASB).

Timothy's mother raised him to know the "sacred writings"—today's Old Testament. That was no easy task in a time when literate women were rare and a household copy of the scriptures even more so. It's unlikely that Timothy's Greek father helped. (Timothy was uncircumcised according to Acts 16:3, indicating that the family did not have a Jewish identity.) Scholars suggest that Eunice made sure Timothy had a tutor or recited what she herself had been taught. In any case, she was intentional about teaching her son God's Word because those writings would prepare him for the message of the Messiah.

Today, parents have the benefit of the New Testament and its commentary and explanation of the words Timothy would have read. Wise parents will "bring [their children] up in the training and instruction of the Lord" (Ephesians 6:4 NIV) by using the entire handbook He has provided.

PRAY:

Author of life, thank You for the full message of salvation in Jesus that has been recorded for us and future generations!

GROWING WITH THE WORD, PART 2

Read 2 Timothy 3:10–17

KEY VERSE:
All Scripture is inspired by God and beneficial for teaching, for rebuke, for correction, for training in righteousness.
2 TIMOTHY 3:16 NASB

CONTEMPLATE:

- What is the source of all scripture?

- How are each of scripture's four uses different?

- Is it still useful for our spiritual growth today even though it's thousands of years old?

APPLY:

Some modern writers have suggested that the Old Testament's relevance has been lost and that we should just focus on the New Testament. But in today's Key Verse, we see a different view about "the sacred writings" (2 Timothy 3:15 NASB). Paul declares the scripture to be useful in four ways, all of which are for our spiritual growth. His conviction lay in the fact of the origin of the writing, namely, the breath of God; the author made it authoritative.

Similarly, Jesus looked to the Old Testament as trustworthy and inspired. Not only did He quote it extensively, but after His resurrection, two followers had the privilege of the greatest Bible study imaginable: "Then beginning with Moses and with all the Prophets, He explained to them the things written about Himself in all the Scriptures" (Luke 24:27 NASB). The Old Testament is filled with Jesus!

But what of the Law, from which believers are set free (Romans 7:4)? It also plays a part in the plan of salvation. As Paul explained, "the Law has become our guardian [or tutor] to lead us to Christ" (Galatians 3:24 NASB) by revealing the truth about ourselves. "So the trouble is not with the law, for it is spiritual and good. The trouble is with me, for I am all too human, a slave to sin" (Romans 7:14 NLT). The Law's purpose was to point to a Savior, not to become a means of salvation without Him. The same is true still.

PRAY:

Gracious Lord, I rejoice in the handbook You have created for us to draw closer to You!

GROWING WITH THE WORD, PART 3

Read Colossians 3:12–17

KEY VERSE:

Let the word of Christ dwell in you richly,
teaching and admonishing one another in all
wisdom, singing psalms and hymns and spiritual
songs, with thankfulness in your hearts to God.
COLOSSIANS 3:16 ESV

CONTEMPLATE:

- What does Paul desire about "the word of Christ" for the Colossians?

- What kinds of activities does "the word of Christ" lead to?

APPLY:

As we've seen, the Old Testament was filled with the message of the coming Messiah, though often obscured, and that the scriptures are still useful for "training in righteousness" (2 Timothy 3:16 NASB) because "the LORD gives wisdom; from his mouth come knowledge and understanding" (Proverbs 2:6 ESV).

In the New Testament, the wisdom of God becomes clearer; the mystery of salvation is revealed, and we gain an understanding of "things into which angels long to look" (1 Peter 1:12 ESV).

As sons of God, we are designed to grow spiritually by "the word of Christ." Paul said, "faith comes from hearing, and hearing through the word of Christ" (Romans 10:17 ESV). That's not only *saving* faith but also *growing* faith.

Jesus made it plain how we can go deeper with Him: "Whoever has my commands and keeps them is the one who loves me. The one who loves me will be loved by my Father, and I too will love them and show myself to them" (John 14:21 NIV). In His wisdom, He'll add trials, challenges, and other training tools, but the foundation of our lives must be built on His Word first. If you've ever tried to put together furniture without the manual, you understand the idea.

We can only become the sons that God called us to be through the teachings, instructions, and explanations we have collected in His manual!

PRAY:
Lord my God, You have called me and also provided for me in Your written Word. Thank You with all my heart!

REASON ISN'T ENOUGH

Read Acts 17:16–34

KEY VERSES:

Now while Paul was waiting for them at Athens, his spirit was provoked within him as he saw that the city was full of idols. So he reasoned in the synagogue with the Jews and the devout persons, and in the marketplace every day with those who happened to be there.

ACTS 17:16–17 ESV

CONTEMPLATE:

- What was Paul provoked by in the city of Athens?

- What did he do in response to a city filled with idols?

APPLY:

Paul, a Hellenistic Jew from Tarsus, had an impressive lineage—"a Hebrew of Hebrews; in regard to the law, a Pharisee" (Philippians 3:5 NIV). He was also well educated in Greek philosophy and poetry which he sometimes referenced. Knowing Paul's background adds context to our studies.

On his second missionary journey, Paul visited Athens, the birthplace of Socrates and Plato, whose inhabitants had a reputation: "Now all the Athenians and the foreigners who lived there would spend their time in nothing except telling or hearing something new" (Acts 17:21 esv). Eventually, some philosophers invited him to address the elite body of thinkers called the Areopagus, where he included quotes from two Greek philosophers in his presentation of the gospel. There were three reactions: "When they heard about the resurrection of the dead, some of them *sneered*, but others said, '*We want to hear you again* on this subject.' At that, Paul left the Council. Some of the people became followers of Paul and *believed*" (Acts 17:32–34 niv). Shortly after this, Paul left for Corinth, where he spent a year and a half.

Why is this part of Paul's story important? As we'll see in our next few studies in 1 Corinthians, though Paul communicated wisely, he did not put his trust in his own powers of communication.

PRAY:

Father, give me insight and wisdom to present clearly the importance of the cross of Jesus.

THE FOLLY OF THE CROSS

Read 1 Corinthians 1:17–25

KEY VERSES:

For Christ did not send me to baptize but to preach the gospel, and not with words of eloquent wisdom, lest the cross of Christ be emptied of its power. For the word of the cross is folly to those who are perishing, but to us who are being saved it is the power of God.

1 CORINTHIANS 1:17–18 ESV

CONTEMPLATE:

- What were Paul's calling and purpose?

- What did he avoid doing when sharing the good news of Jesus Christ?

- What words would you use to describe God's power and the power of the cross?

APPLY:

Paul, understanding the centrality of the cross, refused to allow his gospel message to rest simply on the eloquence of his rhetoric or the power of his arguments. "My message and my preaching were not with wise and persuasive words, but with a demonstration of the Spirit's power, so that your faith might not rest on human wisdom, but on God's power" (1 Corinthians 2:4–5 NIV). While in Corinth, Paul's focus was clear: "For I resolved to know nothing while I was with you except Jesus Christ and him crucified" (1 Corinthians 2:2 NIV).

Paul refused to treat the eternal message of salvation like just another human philosophy, propped up by human reason and vulnerable to human argument. He warned believers to be on guard so "no one takes you captive through hollow and deceptive philosophy, which depends on human tradition and the elemental spiritual forces of this world rather than on Christ" (Colossians 2:8 NIV).

PRAY:

Wise and loving Father, guard me against the temptation to add anything of my own to the pure message of the cross!

A STUMBLING BLOCK

Read 1 Corinthians 1:17–25

KEY VERSES:

*For Jews demand signs and Greeks seek
wisdom, but we preach Christ crucified, a
stumbling block to Jews and folly to Gentiles.*
1 CORINTHIANS 1:22–23 ESV

CONTEMPLATE:

- Why did Jews insist on seeing signs from
  heaven?

- How accustomed were the Jews to seeing
  many signs in the Old Testament?

- How accustomed were those who lived during
  Jesus' ministry to seeing signs?

APPLY:

Paul criticized the Jews' insistence on "signs" not
because God doesn't grant them but because the
Jews were never satisfied. The prophets performed
miracles for centuries, and still, many died at the
hands of their own people.

Jesus rebuked the Jews of His day for following
the pattern of their forefathers: "You consent to the
deeds of your fathers, for they killed [the prophets],

and you build their tombs" (Luke 11:48 esv). When they demanded a sign of His own authority, He answered, "A wicked and adulterous generation asks for a sign! But none will be given it except the sign of the prophet Jonah" (Matthew 12:39 niv), meaning His death and resurrection. Even when He provided that very sign, the Jews demanded more: "Let him come down now from the cross, and we will believe in him" (Matthew 27:42 esv).

The irony is that if He had come down, they would have had nothing to believe in. He would not have been their Messiah without the cross, and they couldn't see it. The Old Testament clearly promised a Savior who would suffer and die, but the Jews stubbornly relied on their own intellect, which blinded them to it.

Even His closest followers were slow to grasp the resurrection until He "opened their minds so they could understand the Scriptures. He told them, 'This is what is written: The Messiah will suffer and rise from the dead on the third day'" (Luke 24:45–46 niv).

PRAY:
Thank You, Father in heaven, for giving me the only sign that really matters!

FOOLISH AND WEAK

Read 1 Corinthians 1:26–31

KEY VERSE:

But God chose the foolish things of the world
to shame the wise; God chose the weak
things of the world to shame the strong.
1 CORINTHIANS 1:27 NIV

CONTEMPLATE:

- Why would God have any interest in shaming
  the wise or choosing the weak?

- The Greeks valued wisdom: How can that be
  an impediment to knowing God?

APPLY:

Not many people would enjoy being called "foolish"
and "weak" (verse 27 NIV) not to mention "lowly" and
"despised" (verse 28 NIV). There's not much point in
doing a deeper word study either—it doesn't get any
better! But in today's passage, Paul argues that it's
a blessing and an important part of God's plan for
all humankind as announced in the scriptures: "As
the Scriptures say, 'I will destroy the wisdom of the
wise and discard the intelligence of the intelligent'"
(1 Corinthians 1:19 NLT, quoting Isaiah 29:14). God
"opposes the proud but gives grace to the humble"

(1 Peter 5:5 ESV, quoting Proverb 3:34).

In the gospel, God turns "the world upside down" (Acts 17:6 ESV) for those who deny Him, but He hits the reset button for all who believe. After the fall, humankind "did not see fit to acknowledge God" (Romans 1:28 NASB) and hit the accelerator to create a world without Him: "For although they knew God, they neither glorified him as God nor gave thanks to him, but their thinking became futile and their foolish hearts were darkened. Although they claimed to be wise, they became fools" (Romans 1:21–22 NIV). Thus, God chose the "things counted as nothing at all, and used them to bring to nothing what the world considers important" (1 Corinthians 1:28 NLT). He's shaming the wise and the strong of this world by using the worst He can find: you and me!

PRAY:
I praise You, holy Father, because I'm happy to be a fool that brings You glory!

WISDOM FOR THE MATURE

Read 1 Corinthians 2:1–11

KEY VERSES:

We do, however, speak a message of wisdom among the mature, but not the wisdom of this age or of the rulers of this age, who are coming to nothing. No, we declare God's wisdom, a mystery that has been hidden and that God destined for our glory before time began.

1 CORINTHIANS 2:6–7 NIV

CONTEMPLATE:

- What is the "mystery" of God Paul is referring to in this passage?

- Who does Paul look for to share the deeper things of God?

APPLY:

If you've ever been asked by a child where babies come from, you'll understand something of Paul's dilemma among the Corinthians. He wanted to impart so much about the mystery of God revealed in Christ but was held back by their spiritual immaturity.

Although salvation through Jesus had been "made known through the prophetic writings by the command of the eternal God" (Romans 16:26 NIV), people could still not comprehend it. Some were hardened, some found it foolish, and some, like the Corinthian church, were stubbornly immature in their faith. They weren't growing up, and for Paul, that was frustrating: "When I was with you I couldn't talk to you as I would to spiritual people. I had to talk as though you belonged to this world or as though you were infants in Christ" (1 Corinthians 3:1 NLT). Being a baby isn't wrong, but remaining one is a problem: "like newborn babies, long for the pure milk of the word, so that by it you may grow in respect to salvation" (1 Peter 2:2 NASB).

For Paul, preaching the gospel wasn't merely about evangelism. "[Jesus] we proclaim, warning everyone and teaching everyone with all wisdom, that we may present everyone mature in Christ" (Colossians 1:28 ESV). Maturity is the hope of all good parents for their children.

PRAY:

Sovereign Lord, forgive me for my immaturity that comes either through stubbornness or complacency!

LEARNING TO SPEAK SPIRITUAL WORDS

Read 1 Corinthians 2:12–16

KEY VERSES:

*Now we have not received the spirit of the world,
but the Spirit who is from God, so that we may
know the things freely given to us by God. We
also speak these things, not in words taught by
human wisdom, but in those taught by the Spirit,
combining spiritual thoughts with spiritual words.*

1 CORINTHIANS 2:12–13 NASB

CONTEMPLATE:

- What characteristics would you expect of "the spirit of the world"?

- What has God freely given us?

- Who teaches us to communicate spiritual ideas?

APPLY:

Think about Paul's experience in Athens and how he proclaimed the gospel before the leading philosophers—only a few believed although Paul's presentation was one of the most profound recorded in the Bible. That experience framed his time in Corinth and also gives us insight into today's passage.

Paul wrote 1 Corinthians to a growing though immature congregation. And although he did speak a message of wisdom, he emphasized that it was not something he or any other man had invented. Unlike the Greek philosophers who built up human reason alone, Paul drew from another source entirely. Like Paul, we are connected to that source and can experience the promise of Jesus to His followers: "I will give you words and wisdom that none of your adversaries will be able to resist or contradict" (Luke 21:15 NIV).

Being "taught by the Spirit" means both a learning process *and* divine inspiration. Jesus combined these two ideas when He promised, "the Holy Spirit, whom the Father will send in my name, will teach you all things and will remind you of everything I have said to you" (John 14:26 NIV). Paul knew the scriptures well and the teaching of Jesus, but he also knew that to speak spiritually he had to listen and learn from the Spirit.

PRAY:

Keep me ever attentive to the voice of Your Holy Spirit, O Lord, as I study Your living Word.

BE A FOOL FOR A GOOD REASON

Read 1 Corinthians 3

KEY VERSES:

Don't you realize that all of you together are the temple of God and that the Spirit of God lives in you? God will destroy anyone who destroys this temple. For God's temple is holy, and you are that temple. Stop deceiving yourselves. If you think you are wise by this world's standards, you need to become a fool to be truly wise. For the wisdom of this world is foolishness to God.

1 CORINTHIANS 3:16–19 NLT

CONTEMPLATE:

- In what ways have you seen "worldly wisdom" result in real foolishness, according to God?

- What are some ways you can test the authenticity of real wisdom?

APPLY:

As we continue to look at 1 Corinthians, we need to ask why Paul spent so much of the first three chapters discussing the difference between godly wisdom and worldly wisdom. If a Bible writer spends that much time on a theme, there must be a good reason!

The context of Paul's discourse on wisdom was factions and divisions within the church: "Each one of you says, 'I follow Paul,' or 'I follow Apollos,' or 'I follow Cephas,' or 'I follow Christ'" (1 Corinthians 1:12 ESV). Thinking themselves superior, each camp boasted like an old kung fu movie: "My master can beat up your master!" Corinth was a competitive city politically, economically, and athletically (home of the Isthmian Games), and the church had become contaminated by rivalries. Not surprisingly, Paul had to strongly denounce this destructive worldview they called "wisdom."

We can do the same thing today if we allow rivalries to divide us rather than obeying the imperatives to "fervently love one another from the heart" (1 Peter 1:22 NASB), and "make every effort to keep yourselves united in the Spirit, binding yourselves together with peace" (Ephesians 4:3 NLT). We are not to live "like mere humans" (1 Corinthians 3:3 NIV), but as God's holy people —even if it means appearing to be fools!

PRAY:

Father, guard my mind against human reason alone when it would keep me from following Your written Word!

THE MYSTERY OF THE CHURCH, PART 1

Read Ephesians 3:1–13

KEY VERSE:

This mystery is that through the gospel the Gentiles are heirs together with Israel, members together of one body, and sharers together in the promise in Christ Jesus.
EPHESIANS 3:6 NIV

CONTEMPLATE:

- What was the mystery Paul says God had revealed to him?

- Why would including Gentiles in the offer of salvation be such a big deal?

APPLY:

As we've discussed, knowing the context of a passage can make all the difference. What seems obvious to us today—the availability of the gospel to all humankind—was a mystery to the Jews of Jesus and Paul's day.

From the fall of man to the Tower of Babel, humankind repeatedly rejected God. Then, the Bible concentrates on a nation that God created from one man—Abraham—to whom He promised: "I will make you into a great nation, and I will bless you" (Genesis 12:2 NIV). His descendants were chosen "to be the people of [God's] inheritance" (Deuteronomy 4:20 NIV). It's important to note that God *created* a nation for Himself; He did not select one from those that existed. Thus, everyone outside of Abraham's lineage (the Gentiles) were "excluded from the people of Israel, and strangers to the covenants of the promise, having no hope and without God in the world" (Ephesians 2:12 NASB), and that a "wall of hostility" (Ephesians 2:14 NLT) separated Jew and Gentile.

But in mercy, God had also promised Abraham "through your offspring all nations on earth will be blessed" (Genesis 22:18 NIV). Jesus fulfilled that promise. "You will do more than restore the people of Israel to me. I will make you a light to the Gentiles, and you will bring my salvation to the ends of the earth" (Isaiah 49:6 NLT). In Christ, we all become full heirs of God's covenant and promises.

PRAY:

I thank You, merciful Father, for including me in Your covenant through Jesus!

THE MYSTERY OF THE CHURCH, PART 2

Read Ephesians 3:1–13

KEY VERSES:

I was chosen to explain to everyone this mysterious plan that God, the Creator of all things, had kept secret from the beginning. God's purpose in all this was to use the church to display his wisdom in its rich variety to all the unseen rulers and authorities in the heavenly places. This was his eternal plan, which he carried out through Christ Jesus our Lord.
EPHESIANS 3:9–11 NLT

CONTEMPLATE:

- Who does Paul say he was called to preach to?

- Regarding the mystery of the church, what is God's purpose?

- What are "rulers and authorities in the heavenly places"?

APPLY:

The Bible is a history of the natural and supernatural worlds and their relationship. The natural world is what we experience through our senses, and the "heavenly places" are an unseen realm of spiritual beings (*elohim*), of whom God is supreme (*Elohim*). Not all people follow God, and likewise not all *elohim* are on His side. Paul faced human opposition but emphasized that "we do not wrestle against flesh and blood, but against the rulers, against the authorities, against the cosmic powers over this present darkness, against the spiritual forces of evil in the heavenly places" (Ephesians 6:12 ESV).

Commonly called "spiritual warfare," we need to be aware of its reality, though not afraid since Jesus "disarmed the powers and authorities" and "made a public spectacle of them, *triumphing* over them by the cross" (Colossians 2:15 NIV). In addition, God "raised [Jesus] from the dead and seated him at his right hand in the heavenly places, far above all rule and authority and power and dominion" (Ephesians 1:20–21 ESV). As the body of Christ, we were created to "display [God's] wisdom in its rich variety" not just on earth, but in the "heavenly places" too.

PRAY:
*I praise You Lord for Your victory over all
things that would separate us from You.*

A CONTINUOUS FOUNDATION

Read Matthew 7:21–29

KEY VERSES:

"Therefore everyone who hears these words of mine and puts them into practice is like a wise man who built his house on the rock. The rain came down, the streams rose, and the winds blew and beat against that house; yet it did not fall, because it had its foundation on the rock."

MATTHEW 7:24–25 NIV

CONTEMPLATE:

- What does Jesus say qualifies us to be called wise?

- In this parable, does the wise man face less trouble than the foolish man?

- What was the foolish man's outcome in this parable?

APPLY:

Some parables can be tough to grasp when looking at them from a modern perspective. Today's reading is not one of those! And you don't have to be in the construction industry to get the point Jesus is making.

A solid foundation for a house is just common sense. Even if you live along the coast where houses are built on pilings, the goal is to hit rock by going deep. The same is true for our spiritual lives.

There is, however, an interesting grammatical usage in today's passage. Jesus uses the present tense to qualify the subject—"everyone who *hears* these words of mine and *puts* them into practice"—then He equates those people to a man who "*built* his house on the rock" which is past tense. How can someone who *does* something be like someone who *did* something?

A building's foundation is a continuous thing. Our houses only work because the foundation keeps doing its job, providing ongoing stability. Obedience works in a similar way, allowing us to expect ongoing spiritual stability in the face of the inevitable tests of life. While God will never abandon His children, last year's obedience isn't a guarantee for today's walk of faith.

PRAY:

God, keep me ever laying the solid foundation of a life of obedience in Christ.

A POSITIVE LOOP

Read Colossians 1:1–14

KEY VERSES:

We continually ask God to fill you with the knowledge of his will through all the wisdom and understanding that the Spirit gives, so that you may live a life worthy of the Lord and please him in every way: bearing fruit in every good work, growing in the knowledge of God,
COLOSSIANS 1:9–10 NIV

CONTEMPLATE:

- What was on Paul's heart for these believers?

- Where do wisdom and understanding come from?

- What does a life "worthy of the Lord" look like?

APPLY:

As we saw in our last study, it's the practice or habit of living by the Word of God that demonstrates wisdom, not simply the collection of insights. While the wisdom from above does enlighten our minds, its goal is to change our lives. We see that combination in today's Key Verses: knowledge and understanding of God's will can lead to a life that pleases Him. That, in turn, produces fruit which leads back to knowing more about God. It's a positive loop of knowing, doing, and knowing more.

Even Jesus—the embodiment of wisdom—experienced this loop. At twelve years old, Jesus accompanied His family on their annual trip to Jerusalem. When they left, he stayed behind. Three days later, His alarmed parents "found Him in the temple, sitting in the midst of the teachers, both listening to them and asking them questions. And all who heard Him were amazed at His understanding and His answers" (Luke 2:46–47 NASB). The remainder of Jesus' youth is described in a single fascinating comment: "And Jesus kept increasing in wisdom and stature, and in favor with God and people" (Luke 2:52 NASB).

Jesus increased in wisdom, even as God in the flesh, and set an eternal example for all believers.

PRAY:

Open my eyes, Lord, that I may see and understand and obey Your will and draw closer to You.

OUTSIDERS

Read Colossians 4:1–6

KEY VERSES:

Walk in wisdom toward outsiders, making the best use of the time. Let your speech always be gracious, seasoned with salt, so that you may know how you ought to answer each person.
COLOSSIANS 4:5–6 ESV

CONTEMPLATE:

- Who or what is an outsider?

- In what ways are we to make the best use of our opportunities with outsiders?

- How should we talk to those who are not of the same Christian worldview?

APPLY:

In New Testament times there weren't churches on every corner. There may have been various congregations that met in homes (1 Corinthians 16:19, Philemon 1:2) but "the church" in most cities viewed itself, and functioned, as one body. Christians were obviously in the minority among Greek pagans but sometimes also in large Jewish communities. Believers had to be wise in how they navigated the society that surrounded them.

Sometimes the church enjoyed "having favor with all the people" as in Jerusalem after Pentecost where, "the Lord added to their number day by day those who were being saved" (Acts 2:47 ESV). But often it was the opposite, as in Thessalonica: "the Jews were jealous, and taking some wicked men of the rabble, they formed a mob, set the city in an uproar, and attacked the house of Jason, seeking to bring them out to the crowd" (Acts 17:5 ESV).

Despite the danger of persecution, Paul's instruction to be wise toward outsiders wasn't primarily about avoiding trouble. It was about making the gospel credible by our example. Peter similarly reminded his audience, "Always be prepared to give an answer to everyone who asks you to give the reason for the hope that you have. But do this with gentleness and respect, keeping a clear conscience" (1 Peter 3:15–16 NIV). The world has the right to judge our message by our behavior.

PRAY:

Father, grant me wisdom to live and to speak wisely, so unbelievers will see Your Spirit working.

OPPORTUNITIES

Read Ephesians 5:1–21

KEY VERSES:

So then, be careful how you walk, not as unwise people but as wise, making the most of your time, because the days are evil. Therefore do not be foolish, but understand what the will of the Lord is.
EPHESIANS 5:15–17 NASB

CONTEMPLATE:

- What does Paul point to as the reason to live wisely?

- What are we to avoid or pursue?

APPLY:

Paul had similar concerns for all the churches he shepherded. Today's passage is similar to his directions to the Colossians, whom he had not yet met, but with a darker tone—likely from his own experience in Ephesus.

As was his custom, Paul entered the local synagogue on his first visit to Ephesus, "and for three months spoke boldly, reasoning and persuading them about the kingdom of God" (Acts 19:8 ESV). Some believed, but others began to malign the gospel. So, Paul "withdrew from them and took the disciples with him, reasoning daily in the hall of Tyrannus. This continued for two years, so that all the residents of Asia heard the word of the Lord, both Jews and Greeks" (Acts 19:9–10 ESV). Paul turned the Jews' rejection into a unique opportunity.

During those two years, many converted as "fear fell upon them all, and the name of the Lord Jesus was extolled" (Acts 19:17 ESV). But fierce opposition grew from a silversmith named Demetrius "who had a large business manufacturing silver shrines of the Greek goddess Artemis" (Acts 19:24 NLT). As the gospel threatened his income, he stirred up a mob that could have ended badly if a cool-headed city official hadn't intervened. Knowing his opportunity in Ephesus had come to a close, Paul left for Macedonia.

Like the Ephesians, as our "days are evil" we need to be wise about every opportunity for the gospel.

PRAY:
Lord, I want to know Your will, making the most of the opportunities You give me for the gospel.

PERSECUTION

Read Matthew 10:5–20

KEY VERSE:

*"Behold, I am sending you out as sheep
in the midst of wolves, so be wise as
serpents and innocent as doves."*
MATTHEW 10:16 ESV

CONTEMPLATE:

- What characteristics do the four animals in this verse personify?

- How is a "serpent" a metaphor for wisdom?

APPLY:

Animal metaphors have always been part of human language and appear throughout the Bible: lions are strong, heifers are stubborn, and eagles are swift. In today's Key Verse, Jesus used four animals symbolically to emphasize His meaning.

At a key point in His ministry, Jesus sent out His twelve disciples to proclaim a simple message: "The kingdom of heaven is at hand" (Matthew 10:7 ESV). And despite being given the authority to heal the sick and even raise the dead, they would still be like "sheep in the midst of wolves" (Matthew 10:16 ESV). They would attract opposition from both religious and secular sources and be "dragged before" courts, governors, and kings (Matthew 10:18–19 ESV).

Because they would be so vulnerable, these situations would require the disciples to be wise. In the Greek, *phronimos* means "practically wise" or "discerning." Ironically, the serpent personified those things even in the garden of Eden! "Now the serpent was more crafty than any other beast" (Genesis 3:1 ESV). The Hebrew for *crafty* is elsewhere translated as "shrewd" or "sensible." For good or ill, the serpent was a thinker, and Jesus wanted His disciples to take note.

But in a possible counterbalance to the historically problematic serpent, Jesus invoked the dove, which is "innocent" (*akeraios*) or *unmixed with contaminants* and *without guile*. No matter how shrewd they must become, the disciples could not afford to play the world's game if their message was to be true to the one who sent them.

PRAY:
*Wise Father, teach me to be practical
and discerning but also gentle and
innocent for the sake of Your gospel.*

AUTHORITY, PART 1

Read Titus 2

KEY VERSES:

Teach slaves to be subject to their masters in everything, to try to please them, not to talk back to them, and not to steal from them, but to show that they can be fully trusted, so that in every way they will make the teaching about God our Savior attractive.

TITUS 2:9–10 NIV

CONTEMPLATE:

- What was the historical context of Paul's instruction to Titus?

- What is the point Paul is making about wise behavior toward authority?

APPLY:

Historical context is critical in today's passage since it touches on a subject that has changed drastically since ancient times. We need to look for the principles that will be useful today.

Thankfully, legal slavery does not exist in the West anymore. But for thousands of years, indebted servitude was an economic fact of life. The scriptures taught the fair treatment of slaves (Colossians 3:11) and encouraged obtaining freedom when possible (1 Corinthians 7:21). But what if you were stuck under someone else's authority? As always, Paul's main concern was the gospel. He commanded that slaves show "they can be fully trusted" because it would make "the teaching about God our Savior attractive." Paul wasn't unsympathetic to the "yoke of slavery" (1 Timothy 6:1 NIV). But his point was that even from a position of weakness, we can serve God.

Joseph was sold into slavery by his own brothers but honored God, and "Potiphar put him in charge of his household, and he entrusted to his care everything he owned" (Genesis 39:4 NIV). Later, Pharaoh said, "there is no one so discerning and wise as you. You shall be in charge of my palace, and all my people are to submit to your orders" (Genesis 41:39–40 NIV). Joseph never sought advancement. He simply acted faithfully, and the God of Israel was made known to an entire nation.

PRAY:

Faithful Father, teach me to be faithful and trustworthy in my work, for Your name's sake.

AUTHORITY, PART 2

Read Ephesians 6:1–9

Key Verse:

*And masters, do the same things to them,
and give up threatening, knowing that
both their Master and yours is in heaven,
and there is no partiality with Him.*
Ephesians 6:9 nasb

Contemplate:

- How are those who are in authority over people to act toward those they direct?

- Is there any room for abusive or threatening behavior in a Christian leader?

- What should be the motivation of a believer who is in authority?

Apply:

The epistles of the New Testament explain both the *how* and the *why* we should act as "ambassadors for Christ" (2 Corinthians 5:20 esv), addressing both sides of human relationships—husbands and wives, children and parents, slave and free. While instructions to bondservants may not completely translate to modern-day employment, the warning to those in authority over people is still applicable.

Those who are given authority, whether in the marketplace, the military, or the church have clear responsibilities. When Paul tells masters to treat slaves "in the same way" (Ephesians 6:9 NLT), he's emphasizing that it's not just the slave who is "working for the Lord" (Ephesians 6:7 NLT). These two have a mutual Master in heaven who "will reward each one of us for the good we do, whether we are slaves or free" (Ephesians 6:8 NLT).

Jesus went so far as to redefine authority. "You know that the rulers in this world *lord it* over their people, and officials flaunt their authority over those under them. But among you it will be different" (Mark 10:42–43 NLT). Your position may put you over people, but it doesn't make you superior; it makes you more accountable! Those who are in authority should take to heart what the psalmist said: "Now therefore, O kings, be wise; be warned, O rulers of the earth. Serve the LORD with fear, and rejoice with trembling" (Psalm 2:10–11 ESV).

PRAY:

Sovereign Lord, in whatever position You place me, may I be a faithful witness to Your great salvation.

A PROPER SELF VIEW, PART 1

Read Romans 12

KEY VERSE:

Live in harmony with one another. Do not be haughty, but associate with the lowly. Never be wise in your own sight.

ROMANS 12:16 ESV

CONTEMPLATE:

- Why is harmony between believers important?

- Who qualifies as "the lowly" today? Do you know any "lowly" people?

- How would you paraphrase being "wise in your own sight"?

APPLY:

Sometimes verses speak for themselves, making them great to memorize and share. But even those verses need context from the fuller passage, perhaps even the entire book, as we saw with Ecclesiastes.

Most of the New Testament comes to us as letters which would have been read aloud to a congregation. As part of your Bible study approach, try listening to a passage being read in a Bible app and see if it offers a different perspective than reading silently.

Romans 12 is a turning point in Paul's letter, moving from a theological and explanatory tone to an impassioned plea for godly living. It implores believers to offer themselves as a "living sacrifice" (verse 1) to God, not to earn salvation but because of it, and to not conform to this world. To the mature in Christ, Paul warns them, "not to think more highly of himself than he ought to think; but to think so as to have sound judgment" (Romans 12:3 NASB). Be self-aware, just not puffed up. Paul knew that a clear indication of an exaggerated self-opinion is disassociation with the "lowly"—those who can't offer anything in return for attention. We make a serious mistake when we don't regard those at the "bottom" worth serving, as Jesus made clear: "I tell you the truth, when you refused to help the *least of these my brothers and sisters*, you were refusing to help me" (Matthew 25:45 NLT).

PRAY:
*Open my eyes, Father, to see those who are
in need and to serve You through them.*

A PROPER SELF VIEW, PART 2

Read 2 Corinthians 10

KEY VERSES:

We do not dare to classify or compare ourselves with some who commend themselves. When they measure themselves by themselves and compare themselves with themselves, they are not wise. We, however, will not boast beyond proper limits, but will confine our boasting to the sphere of service God himself has assigned to us, a sphere that also includes you.

2 CORINTHIANS 10:12–13 NIV

CONTEMPLATE:

- What does it mean for someone to "commend" himself?

- What did Paul do in contrast to those who boasted about themselves?

- What "sphere of service" has God assigned to you?

APPLY:

Paul spent a fair amount of energy defending his flocks. He told the Ephesian church, "I know that after I leave, savage wolves will come in among you and will not spare the flock. Even from your own number men will arise and distort the truth in order to draw away disciples after them" (Acts 20:29–30 NIV). Self-centered and greedy false teachers were just as rampant in Paul's day as they are in ours.

As we studied yesterday, the tone of a letter can help clarify a passage. Paul begins this section ironically, "We do not dare to classify or compare ourselves. . ." and then goes ahead and does it! He's answering fools according to their folly (Proverb 26:5) to highlight their absurd mutual admiration society. They were "not wise" for exchanging pats on the back and calling it credibility.

Paul had real credibility, but he wasn't interested in self-promotion. He took his own advice "not to think more highly of himself than he ought to think" (Romans 12:3 NASB). That meant simply being honest with what God had called him to do and letting "someone else praise you, and not your own mouth; an outsider, and not your own lips" (Proverbs 27:2 NIV).

PRAY:

Father, Your opinion alone matters.
Help me to simply be faithful to Your calling.

SOLOMON'S PRAYER

Read 1 Kings 3:7–14

KEY VERSES:

"Your servant is here among the people you have chosen, a great people, too numerous to count or number. So give your servant a discerning heart to govern your people and to distinguish between right and wrong. For who is able to govern this great people of yours?" The Lord was pleased that Solomon had asked for this. So God said to him, "Since you have asked for. . .discernment in administering justice, I will do what you have asked. I will give you a wise and discerning heart, so that there will never have been anyone like you, nor will there ever be."

1 KINGS 3:8–12 NIV

CONTEMPLATE:

- What was Solomon's attitude toward his new role as king?

- Why was God pleased with Solomon's request?

- What did God do in addition to granting Solomon's request?

Apply:

Solomon had been king for a few years before God appeared to him in a vision—enough time to see how hard the job was! His father, David, had established the royal line after succeeding Saul, but Solomon still had significant challenges. As the youngest son of David, he faced opposition from his elder brother, Adonijah, and from hostile nations eager to test a young king.

But Solomon had been chosen by God to "build a house for my Name. He will be my son, and I will be his father. And I will establish the throne of his kingdom over Israel forever" (1 Chronicles 22:10 NIV). Solomon's request for wisdom was pleasing to God because it showed his dependence on God to do the job He had assigned. Likewise, we are chosen in Christ, and we embody that fact by calling on Him for wisdom and strength to fulfill our calling.

Pray:

Father, I want to please You by what I desire; ignore my pleas for worthless things!

SOLOMON'S REPUTATION

Read 1 Kings 3:16–28

KEY VERSES:

Then [Solomon] said, "Cut the living child in two, and give half to one woman and half to the other!" Then the woman who was the real mother of the living child, and who loved him very much, cried out, "Oh no, my lord! Give her the child—please do not kill him!" But the other woman said, "All right, he will be neither yours nor mine; divide him between us!" Then the king said, "Do not kill the child, but give him to the woman who wants him to live, for she is his mother!" When all Israel heard the king's decision, the people were in awe of the king, for they saw the wisdom God had given him for rendering justice.

1 KINGS 3:25–28 NLT

CONTEMPLATE:

- How did Solomon know what the mother's reaction would be?

- What was the nation's reaction to his judgment?

Apply:

The first story of Solomon's God-given wisdom was as dramatic as it was unlikely. How did two prostitutes even get an audience with the king? Apparently, the case was so puzzling to the lower courts that it ended up in front of the king, as Moses had intended: "And [trusted men] judged the people at all times. Any hard case they brought to Moses, but any small matter they decided themselves" (Exodus 18:26 esv). This case wasn't hard—it was impossible. Imagine the murmurs as the women argued and the breathlessness when Solomon asked for a sword! Was he going to be an unpredictable and violent king like Saul rather than a shepherd like his father?

But "wisdom is proved right by her deeds" (Matthew 11:19 niv) and the results of this case established Solomon's reputation before the entire kingdom. That was just the beginning. Other nations would soon hear of this wise king.

Pray:

Father, grant me wisdom when faced with tough choices so that Your reputation spreads, not mine.

FAME GROWS

Read 1 Kings 10

KEY VERSES:

When the queen of Sheba heard about the fame of Solomon and his relationship to the LORD, she came to test Solomon with hard questions. . . . Solomon answered all her questions; nothing was too hard for the king to explain to her. When the queen of Sheba saw all the wisdom of Solomon and the palace he had built, the food on his table, the seating of his officials, the attending servants in their robes, his cupbearers, and the burnt offerings he made at the temple of the LORD, she was overwhelmed.
1 KINGS 10:1, 3–5 NIV

CONTEMPLATE:

- What was the queen's purpose in visiting Solomon?

- What was her response to what she heard and saw?

APPLY:

Many years into his reign, Solomon received a visit from the Queen of Sheba (or "Queen of the South," Matthew 12:42; most likely southern Arabia). Monarchs had come before, but this visit made front page news! Her gifts were unheard of. In addition to mountains of gold and jewels, "Never again were so many spices brought in as those the queen of Sheba gave to King Solomon" (1 Kings 10:10 NIV). But she got more than she gave and was "overwhelmed." Her reaction?

"How happy your people must be! How happy your officials, who continually stand before you and hear your wisdom! Praise be to the LORD your God, who has delighted in you and placed you on the throne of Israel. Because of the LORD's eternal love for Israel, he has made you king to maintain justice and righteousness" (1 Kings 10:8–9 NIV).

Solomon had become a testimony to the world of God's love and a gift to Israel to "maintain justice and righteousness." But as we'll see next, the wisdom Solomon shared with others did not always apply to himself.

PRAY:

May my words and my life point always to
Your lovingkindness and goodness, O Lord.

SOLOMON'S DOWNFALL

Read 1 Kings 11:1–15

KEY VERSES:

King Solomon, however, loved many foreign women besides Pharaoh's daughter—Moabites, Ammonites, Edomites, Sidonians and Hittites. They were from nations about which the Lord had told the Israelites, "You must not intermarry with them, because they will surely turn your hearts after their gods." Nevertheless, Solomon held fast to them in love.

1 KINGS 11:1–2 NIV

CONTEMPLATE:

- What caused Solomon's spiritual and political downfall?

- How would a man of such great wisdom ignore the direct commandment of God?

APPLY:

By all human accounts, King Solomon was a success. "Solomon's wisdom was greater than the wisdom of all the people of the East, and greater than all the wisdom of Egypt. He was wiser than anyone else.... And his fame spread to all the surrounding nations." (1 Kings 4:30–31 NIV).

His forty-year reign brought peace and made Israel rich. But there's no real wisdom without obedience to God's Word. Israelites were forbidden to intermarry with foreign nations because it would lead to idolatry (Deuteronomy 7:3–5). Pretty simple.

But Moses went further: "The king must not take many wives for himself, because they will turn his heart away from the LORD" (Deuteronomy 17:17 NLT). Israel wouldn't even have their first king for 360 years, but just to remove any excuses by those future kings, Moses commanded: "When he sits on the throne as king, he must copy for himself this body of instruction on a scroll in the presence of the Levitical priests. He must always keep that copy with him and read it daily as long as he lives. That way he will learn to fear the LORD his God by obeying all the terms of these instructions and decrees" (Deuteronomy 17:18–19 NLT).

Solomon was granted wisdom by God, but in the end, he abandoned the wisest thing of all: obedience to the written Word.

PRAY:

Gracious God, grant me wisdom, but with it teach me obedience to Your Word.

A LESSON FOR ALL

Read 1 Kings 11:1–15

KEY VERSES:

For when Solomon was old, his wives turned his heart away to follow other gods; and his heart was not wholly devoted to the LORD his God, as the heart of his father David had been. . . . So Solomon did what was evil in the sight of the LORD, and did not follow the LORD fully, as his father David had done.

1 KINGS 11:4, 6 NASB

CONTEMPLATE:

- When did Solomon begin to falter in his relationship to God?

- Who does God compare Solomon to in these verses?

APPLY:

As we've seen in our previous studies, Solomon had a great start but a poor finish. Most scholars believe Solomon repented of his idolatry before his death and wrote Ecclesiastes as his final testimony: "The words of the Preacher, the son of David, king in Jerusalem" (Ecclesiastes 1:1 NASB). Regardless of Solomon's personal relationship with God, the impact of his sin changed history. As punishment, God raised up two previously defeated enemies outside Israel and a new one from inside—Jeroboam, an official in Solomon's own court. Solomon's sin set the kingdom on a path to war.

Solomon, for all his God-given wisdom, made poor choices. He did not remember his own words: "Guard your heart above all else, for it determines the course of your life" (Proverbs 4:23 NLT). Rather, he allowed his heart to become divided. The wives certainly played their part in Solomon's sin, just as temptations come to all of us. But as a descendent of his, who was "greater than Solomon" (Luke 11:31 NIV) said, "Where your treasure is, there will your heart be also" (Luke 12:34 ESV). Solomon lost sight of this critical fact.

We don't need Solomon's wisdom to please God. We just need to guard our hearts according to His Word.

PRAY:
Wise King, show me where I may be making the same mistakes as Solomon and correct me!

UNDERSTANDING PROVERBS

Read Proverbs 1:1–7

KEY VERSES:

Let the wise hear and increase in learning,
and the one who understands obtain guidance,
to understand a proverb and a saying, the
words of the wise and their riddles.
PROVERBS 1:5–6 ESV

CONTEMPLATE:

- What is the point of a proverb?

- Do proverbs need to be "spiritual" to be true?

- How can proverbs be used in daily life?

APPLY:

As we begin digging deeper into the "proverbs of Solomon, son of David, king of Israel" (Proverbs 1:1 ESV) we need to understand what a proverb is and what it isn't. The book of Proverbs belongs to a type of biblical writing known as wisdom literature, (along with Job, Psalms, Ecclesiastes, and Song of Solomon). These books are designed to teach God's perspective through a number of literary vehicles including sayings, songs, poetry, and dialogues; they may employ metaphors, allegories, or even sarcasm!

Most of the sayings we call proverbs were designed to encapsulate a single truth in a memorable way. Collectively, they provide an inspired set of guidelines for wise living that pleases God, explains much about the world, and protects the man who lives by them. They communicate principles rather than promises; general guidance rather than absolute formulas. Sometimes they sound like plain old common sense, and other times they can be esoteric and obscure.

Think of the book of Proverbs as an enormous tool store with aisle after aisle of shiny gadgets and finely crafted utensils. The purpose (meaning) of many will be obvious, but others will need to be explained and demonstrated. But in every case, a tool must be used to increase in skill.

Today's Key Verses admonish those who are wise to learn and become skillful in the tools Solomon left us!

PRAY:
Eternal God, teach me how to apply the proverbs in my own life as well as how to share with others.

APPLYING PROVERBS

Read Proverbs 26:1–5

KEY VERSES:

*Answer not a fool according to his folly, lest you
be like him yourself. Answer a fool according
to his folly, lest he be wise in his own eyes.*

PROVERBS 26:4–5 ESV

CONTEMPLATE:

- How are both of these proverbs true?

- How can you know when to apply them?

APPLY:

Yesterday, we saw how wise sayings are like tools,
each uniquely designed for a job. Today's verses are
a perfect example of how discernment comes into
play when handling these tools correctly. These two
proverbs may sound contradictory to the casual reader
(or critic). But like a claw hammer, you can drive nails
in or pull them out; you simply need to know which
one you want to do.

Jesus employed the wisdom of verse 4 when He
was arrested and brought before king Herod: "When
Herod saw Jesus, he was very glad, for he had long
desired to see him, because he had heard about him,
and he was hoping to see some sign done by him. So

he questioned him at some length, but he made no answer" (Luke 23:8–9 ESV). Jesus would not take part in Herod's foolish desire for entertainment.

Jesus used the second approach to answering a fool when His adversaries tried to trap Him about whether Jews should pay taxes to Caesar: "[Jesus] saw through their duplicity and said to them, 'Show me a denarius. Whose image and inscription are on it?' 'Caesar's,' they replied. He said to them, 'Then give back to Caesar what is Caesar's, and to God what is God's.'. . .And astonished by his answer, they became silent" (Luke 20:23–26 NIV).

Jesus made a public spectacle of their foolishness—doubtless, they no longer felt wise in their own eyes! Like Jesus, if we are discerning, we'll know how to answer effectively.

PRAY:
Help me to be discerning Lord so that I can respond to everyone as You would.

A CALL IGNORED, PART 1

Read Proverbs 1:20–33

KEY VERSES:

Wisdom shouts in the streets. She cries out in the public square. She calls to the crowds along the main street, to those gathered in front of the city gate: "How long, you simpletons, will you insist on being simpleminded? How long will you mockers relish your mocking? How long will you fools hate knowledge? Come and listen to my counsel. I'll share my heart with you and make you wise.

PROVERBS 1:20–23 NLT

CONTEMPLATE:

- What efforts has wisdom made to be heard?
- What kinds of people ignore wisdom's call?

APPLY:

This passage needs a bit of clarification since English has neither feminine nor masculine nouns like Hebrew. English assigns pronouns based on the physical gender of the subject, unless speaking metaphorically, like "she's a fine ship." But in this passage, there's no metaphor, just a grammatical agreement. The Hebrew word for wisdom, *chokhmah*, is a feminine noun requiring a feminine pronoun. The passage is not characterizing wisdom as a woman, unlike Proverbs 9:13 (NLT) which states "the woman named Folly" to alert the reader to the metaphor that follows. In Hebrew, *folly* is also a feminine noun, but that would have been insufficient to bring a woman to mind. Nonetheless, wisdom is personified. . .and pretty active!

Unlike cartoons of a wise man atop a mountain, God's wisdom is not far off. We often talk about pursuing wisdom, when in fact it's the other way around. Wisdom cries out, shouts, even cajoles. Wisdom is looking for us—sadly, to little avail. Why? The passage doesn't mince words: *simpletons* "insist on being simpleminded," *mockers* "relish" in their mocking, and *fools* "hate knowledge"—they don't value wisdom or the God who offers it. In part two of this study, we'll see what happens when these folks get their own way!

PRAY:

Father God, whether wisdom shouts, cries out, or whispers, don't let me fail to hear her voice!

A CALL IGNORED, PART 2

Read Proverbs 1:20–33

KEY VERSES:

*"They rejected my advice and paid no attention
when I corrected them. Therefore they must eat
the bitter fruit of living their own way, choking
on their own schemes. For simpletons turn away
from me—to death. Fools are destroyed by their
own complacency. But all who listen to me will
live in peace, untroubled by fear of harm."*

PROVERBS 1:30–33 NLT

CONTEMPLATE:

- What is the consequence of ignoring wisdom?

- Where do the consequences come from?

- What is the promise to those who embrace wisdom?

APPLY:

There's a pattern in scripture of people who ignore
wisdom and pay the price, starting with Adam and
Eve, followed by their son Cain, and many, many
others. It's all recorded for our benefit, if we will
listen. Actually, if we listen soon enough. Part of
today's longer reading describes a sort of built-in

timeframe for wisdom to be advantageous to us: "When they cry for help, I will not answer. Though they anxiously search for me, they will not find me. For they hated knowledge and chose not to fear the LORD" (Proverbs 1:28–29 NLT).

These anxious cries for help are not about repentance or change, just regret when faced with the consequences of foolish choices. In that respect, wisdom's hands are essentially tied. Like a man who jumps from the top of a tall building and regrets it on the way to the pavement, sometimes it's too late to avoid "the bitter fruit" of bad choices.

Paul repeated this principle: "A man reaps what he sows. Whoever sows to please their flesh, from the flesh will reap destruction; whoever sows to please the Spirit, from the Spirit will reap eternal life" (Galatians 6:7–8 NIV). Consequences come from choices made—accepting wisdom's invitation leads to a life of peace that fools will never know.

PRAY:

Good Father, let me never be among
those who rejected wisdom's calling.

GUARDING THE HEART

Read Proverbs 4:20–27

KEY VERSE:

Guard your heart above all else, for it
determines the course of your life.
PROVERBS 4:23 NLT

CONTEMPLATE:

- What makes the heart so important for those who seek to please God?

- How does one guard the heart?

APPLY:

Knowing and doing don't always go hand in hand. A chain smoker who tells his children not to smoke isn't wrong; he's just not taking his own advice. Likewise, Solomon had much to share about wisdom, though as we've seen, fell short of living by his own advice.

The Hebrew word *lebab,* most often translated as "heart," is always used metaphorically, frequently overlapping with "mind," "soul," or "spirit." As in English, it refers to the deepest part of a man, combining his desires and choices. It can be hardened, stirred, discouraged; evil, noble, upright; tested, faint, thankful; it stores things up and brings things forth. The heart is about as "you" as you can get.

The man who honors God has no allies in this world or even his own flesh. But believers do have an "advocate to help you and be with you forever—the Spirit of truth. . . .you know him, for he lives with you and will be in you" (John 14:16–17 NIV). This is why Paul can advise believers, "Do not conform to the pattern of this world, but be transformed by the renewing of your mind. Then you will be able to test and approve what God's will is—his good, pleasing and perfect will" (Romans 12:2 NIV). To "be transformed" is a passive verb, meaning it happens to you as a result of something else, in this case, renewing the mind by the Spirit of truth. If we "keep in step with the Spirit" (Galatians 5:25 NIV) we never have to guard our hearts alone!

PRAY:

Lord, You've given me a new heart in Christ. Teach me to guard that heart and to listen to Your Spirit.

SELF-CONTROL

Read Proverbs 25:25–28

KEY VERSE:

*A man without self-control is like a city
broken into and left without walls.*
PROVERBS 25:28 ESV

CONTEMPLATE:

- What was the purpose of the city wall in ancient times?

- What would happen if those walls were breached or lay in ruin?

APPLY:

In ancient times, important cities were encircled by high walls for protection. Attacking armies would have to batter down the gates or breach the walls to gain access to the interior.

The most famous walled city in the Bible was Jericho. By God's divine judgment, the Israelites marched and trumpeted and shouted "and the wall fell down flat, so that the [Israelites] went up into the city, every man straight before him, and they captured the city" (Joshua 6:20 ESV). While that situation was of God, the illustration works vividly as a metaphor for today's reading—the enemy of our souls would pour "straight" into our lives if some kind of wall wasn't in place. If "your adversary, the devil, prowls around like a roaring lion, seeking someone to devour" (1 Peter 5:8 NASB), you're going to need protection!

Self-control provides protection from being taken captive by sin, but a man who lacks it is basically a sitting duck. Temptation will find easy access from all directions to his inner man since there's nothing to slow it down. Even if there's only one broken section of the wall, that spot will invite constant attack by the enemy.

These walls of self-control, however, cannot be built by human effort alone since biblical self-control is a "fruit of the Spirit" (Galatians 5:23 ESV). Alone, the enemy's attacks will eventually batter down the stoutest defenses. But believing and walking by God's Spirit will strengthen us against all outside forces, "for God gave us a spirit not of fear but of power and love and self-control" (2 Timothy 1:7 ESV).

PRAY:

Heavenly Father, thank You for Your Spirit,
who strengthens me to exercise self-control.

RESTRAINT

Read Proverbs 29:8–11

KEY VERSE:

A fool gives full vent to his spirit,
but a wise man quietly holds it back.
PROVERBS 29:11 ESV

CONTEMPLATE:

- What does a fool do that a wise man refrains from?

- What advantage does a wise man have by showing restraint?

APPLY:

In previous studies, we've already encountered a character that is common in the book of Proverbs: the fool. The foundation of all fools is explained in Proverbs 1: "The fear of the LORD is the beginning of knowledge, but fools despise wisdom and instruction" (Proverbs 1:7 NIV). The fool prefers his own ways to those of God.

The fool also appears in other wisdom literature where his traits, attitudes, and choices serve to contrast the wise who essentially do the opposite. One of his habits is an inability to control his temper, unlike a man of understanding who maintains his composure and parses his words. A similar proverb says, "Whoever is slow to anger has great understanding, but he who has a hasty temper exalts folly" (Proverbs 14:29 ESV).

In restraint there is power. "One who is slow to anger is better than the mighty, and one who rules his spirit, than one who captures a city" (Proverbs 16:32 NASB). Paul included a specific qualification that an elder not be "quick-tempered" (Titus 1:7 ESV) knowing how damaging that can be for someone who is supposed to be a shepherd.

The fool isn't simply "venting" as we might call it today; he's "giving full vent" to his anger. But therein lies a fine line we need to watch carefully. What we might think of as letting off some steam, in reality, might be stoking the fires even more. We should ask ourselves: Are we working through our anger or excusing it?

PRAY:

Lord, strengthen me to consider my feelings so I do not foolishly allow my temper to speak before I think.

DRINKING, PART 1

Read Proverbs 20:1–5

KEY VERSE:

Wine is a mocker, strong drink a brawler,
and whoever is led astray by it is not wise.
PROVERBS 20:1 ESV

CONTEMPLATE:

- What kind of behavior can intoxication lead to?

- What does "led astray" mean?

- What does the Bible say about alcohol in other passages?

APPLY:

Drinking is a polarizing subject for many Christians. But setting aside personal bias, the Word should speak for itself. As with any topic of personal freedom, we need to survey the whole of scripture to get a balanced understanding.

A thou-shalt-not would settle the question of alcohol pretty quickly, but the Bible never prohibits drinking. It simply stresses the consequences of excess drink.

Wine, like olive oil, was part of the economy and culture of the ancient Middle East. Because of fermentation, alcohol didn't spoil and was often safer to drink than water. Not only was it consumed daily, but it was a prominent part of the Levitical sacrifices. Neither its availability nor sanctified use is an excuse for excess though.

Noah is the first account in scripture of drunkenness. After the flood, he planted a vineyard and "drank of the wine and became drunk and lay uncovered [naked] in his tent" (Genesis 9:21 ESV). Proverbs warns us not to imitate "those who tarry long over wine" because, "In the end it bites like a serpent and stings like an adder" (Proverbs 23:30, 32 ESV). Excess can have dire consequences. As Jesus warned, "But be on your guard, so that your hearts will not be weighed down with dissipation and drunkenness and the worries of life" (Luke 21:34 NASB) and so that you don't miss the day of the Lord.

The question is: Am I being wise with the freedom I've been given, or am I being led astray by my own choices?

PRAY:
Father, guard me against being
tricked by my own freedoms.

DRINKING, PART 2

Read Romans 14

KEY VERSE:

It is good not to eat meat or drink wine or do
anything that causes your brother to stumble.
ROMANS 14:21 ESV

CONTEMPLATE:

- Why would the exercise of your freedom in Christ be a problem for someone else?

- What kind of sacrifice should we be willing to make for the sake of another believer?

APPLY:

In our previous study, we looked at the warnings against drunkenness, not only because it can have severe consequences but because of the distraction it poses. It's not wise to be led astray by any activity that competes with our life in Christ.

But beyond ourselves, there's the question of how our personal freedoms can affect fellow believers. Romans 14 gives us the path of wisdom.

Drinking wine isn't even the main point of Romans 14—it's dietary restrictions and religious observances. The topic of alcohol gets lumped into a larger discussion almost at the end but clearly was among the freedoms we must exercise wisely.

Paul begins the chapter by characterizing believers as either "weak" or "strong" in their faith as determined by their own conscience. A brother who can't get past his Jewish kosher upbringing (even though he's free in Christ) wasn't to judge people like Paul, who was "convinced in the Lord Jesus that nothing is unclean in itself" (Romans 14:14 NASB). Likewise, a believer like Paul wasn't to look down on those who refrained from certain foods because of "a sensitive conscience" (Romans 14:2 NLT). The same applied to "holy" days. "Some think one day is more holy than another day, while others think every day is alike" (Romans 14:5 NLT).

Paul condemned flaunting our freedoms at the expense of our brothers. "Decide instead to live in such a way that you will not cause another believer to stumble and fall" (Romans 14:13 NLT).

PRAY:

*Holy Father, teach me to guard my brothers
by being wise in my own freedom.*

WHO'S TO BLAME?

Read Proverbs 19:1–3

KEY VERSE:

A person's own folly leads to their ruin,
yet their heart rages against the LORD.
PROVERBS 19:3 NIV

CONTEMPLATE:

- Why is it so easy to blame God when we ruin our own lives?

- What does the Bible say about folly and the consequences of our own actions?

APPLY:

Facing the consequences of our own actions is a theme that repeats over and over in the stories of the Bible—as does man's tendency to blame someone else, even God.

After the man and woman disobeyed God's command in the garden of Eden, a conversation follows their transgression in which we glimpse the roots of today's proverb. As God approaches the fearful couple, "they hid from the LORD God among the trees of the garden" (Genesis 3:8 NIV). When God asks Adam pointedly about the forbidden tree, Adam replies, "The woman whom You gave to be with me, she gave me some of the fruit of the tree, and I ate" (Genesis 3:12 NASB). Adam's first instinct was to shift the blame for his folly to both God and his wife!

After wandering in the desert for forty years, Moses reminded the Israelites "you rebelled against the command of the LORD your God and refused to go in. You complained in your tents and said, 'The LORD must hate us'" (Deuteronomy 1:26–27 NLT). The generation that died in the desert tried to find fault with God for their own rebellion.

In Christ, we have mercy and do not always face the full consequences of our actions. But He isn't to blame if we "ruin" our lives by foolish choices. Paul warned believers that "Whoever sows to please their flesh, from the flesh will reap destruction" (Galatians 6:8 NIV). God isn't to blame if our own folly comes back upon us.

PRAY:

Lord, rebuke me if I ever accuse You
when I am the one who's to blame!

SEEKING COUNSEL

Read Proverbs 15:21–23

KEY VERSE:
Plans fail for lack of counsel, but with many advisers they succeed.
PROVERBS 15:22 NIV

CONTEMPLATE:

- What is the point of seeking counsel?
- What qualifies someone to speak into our lives?
- Who in your own life can offer wise counsel?

APPLY:

If you've ever taken on a home project that you've never attempted before (building a deck or remodeling a bathroom), then today's proverb will resonate immediately! Even if your handyman projects are limited to the occasional piece of IKEA furniture, it's far easier to succeed with the input of someone who's "been there, done that." Or maybe you just plowed ahead and tried to figure it out as you went, only to discover that you left out a foundational step that threatened everything. You learned the hard way that, "Enthusiasm without knowledge is no good;

haste makes mistakes" (Proverbs 19:2 NLT).

Most men's lives are filled with complex issues that are too valuable to be left to trial and error. Marriage, children, buying a home, navigating a career. Seeking outside counsel can make a difference in almost every aspect of our lives. "Where there is no guidance, a people falls, but in an abundance of counselors there is safety" (Proverbs 11:14 ESV), and "in an abundance of counselors there is victory" (Proverbs 24:6 NASB).

Of course, the quality of the counsel is based on the quality of the source. Paul warned, "The time is coming when people will not endure sound teaching, but having itching ears they will accumulate for themselves teachers to suit their own passions, and will turn away from listening to the truth and wander off into myths" (2 Timothy 4:3–4 ESV). We need to seek out qualified counselors whose input comes from a solid foundation in the Word of God and a life that demonstrates wisdom.

PRAY:
Help me, Father, to humble myself and ask for guidance from those whom You approve.

LIFELONG LEARNER

Read Proverbs 9:1–9

KEY VERSE:

Give instruction to a wise person and he will become still wiser; teach a righteous person and he will increase his insight.

PROVERBS 9:9 NASB

CONTEMPLATE:

- What characterizes a wise man in today's verse?

- Is there ever a reason to stop learning?

APPLY:

There's an ancient proverb that's not in the Bible but nonetheless rings true: when the student is ready, the teacher will appear. A heart that is humble and a mind that is prepared to learn is like the good soil in Jesus' parable. Good soil is the condition of the heart of the "one who hears the word and understands it. He indeed bears fruit and yields, in one case a hundredfold, in another sixty, and in another thirty" (Matthew 13:23 ESV). Good soil produces results over many, many years.

The connection in today's verse between wisdom and righteousness is often found in the Bible. As you know, real wisdom is about a life that reflects godly character, not simply accumulating knowledge. In the Bible, wisdom is a means to an end, not an achievement in and of itself. "Let not the wise man boast in his wisdom, let not the mighty man boast in his might, let not the rich man boast in his riches, but let him who boasts boast in this, that he *understands and knows me*" (Jeremiah 9:23–24 ESV).

Jesus calls us to be His disciples. The word *disciple* means "learner"—one who "becomes wiser still." And there's no expectation of plateauing since His resources are limitless: "in Him all the fullness of Deity dwells in bodily form" (Colossians 2:9 NASB). We'll never run out of things to learn—not in this life or the next: "this is eternal life, that they *know* you, the only true God, and Jesus Christ whom you have sent" (John 17:3 ESV).

PRAY:

Lord of righteousness, open my heart to learn from You and know You more every day.

FOOLISH WANDERING

Read Proverbs 7

KEY VERSES:

I saw among the simple, I noticed among the young men, a youth who had no sense. He was going down the street near her corner, walking along in the direction of her house at twilight, as the day was fading, as the dark of night set in.

PROVERBS 7:7–9 NIV

CONTEMPLATE:

- What kind of young man is the proverb describing?

- Who is the woman mentioned in the verse?

- Why might the time of day matter?

APPLY:

Different translations try to capture the main thought of a passage in headers that do not appear in the original manuscripts. But like the chapter and verse numbers added many centuries later, these can be useful. The cautionary poem in Proverbs 7 is variously labeled, "Warning Against the Adulteress," "The Lures of the Prostitute," or "Avoid Loose Women." You get the picture.

In a detailed story like this, we can make bullet point observations of the characters' attributes and actions. For example, the man is young and not very bright; he's going down the street of a notorious woman, and he's doing it at twilight. In the following verses, we see the woman confront him, dressed seductively; she's cunning, restless, loud, wayward, brazen, and persuasive. He is no match for her. "All at once he follows her, as an ox goes to the slaughter" (Proverbs 7:22 ESV). The writer's advice: "Let not your heart turn aside to her ways; do not stray into her paths" (Proverbs 7:25 ESV). The folly of the young man lay in not avoiding a temptation he most certainly knew existed.

This story might sound like an unlikely scenario today, with one serious exception: the internet. There are illicit websites seeking to entice the foolish. Wise men do *not* wander past notorious places—they plan another route!

PRAY:
*Father, watch over me and rebuke me if
my carelessness might lead me astray!*

OPINIONS AND BOASTING

Read Proverbs 18:1–8

KEY VERSE:

Fools find no pleasure in understanding but delight in airing their own opinions.

PROVERBS 18:2 NIV

CONTEMPLATE:

- What is the common trait of all biblical "fools"?

- What does a fool find pleasure in when he speaks?

APPLY:

Today's verse is a form of Hebrew poetry known as *antithetic parallelism*, meaning the first and second parts of the verse highlight a contrast between two things. In this case, between what a fool does and does not enjoy.

The fool has no patience to listen or discover something new if it means he might be contradicted in his opinions. Grasping the truth about a subject isn't his goal, preferring to be the center of attention. As the old saying goes, he loves to hear himself talk.

The first cousin of this habit, so to speak, is boasting about himself and his life. Fools are self-aggrandizing—sharpest-guy-in-the-room syndrome—though they are warned, "Do not boast about tomorrow, for you do not know what a day may bring" (Proverbs 27:1 ESV). James expands on this cautionary proverb: "Come now, you who say, 'Today or tomorrow we will go into such and such a town and spend a year there and trade and make a profit'—yet you do not know what tomorrow will bring. What is your life? For you are a mist that appears for a little time and then vanishes" (James 4:13–14 ESV).

The common theme for us who desire to walk in wisdom is just to avoid talking too much. "When there are many words, wrongdoing is unavoidable, but one who restrains his lips is wise" (Proverbs 10:19 NASB). Wisdom is always consistently restrained, not self-asserting, quick to respond, or braggadocious. "Even fools are thought wise if they keep silent, and discerning if they hold their tongues" (Proverbs 17:28 NIV).

PRAY:

Father, set a guard over my mouth and open
my ears to listen and my heart to understand.

THE TONGUE OF THE WISE

Read Proverbs 12:13–19

KEY VERSE:

There is one who speaks rashly like the thrusts of a sword, but the tongue of the wise brings healing.
PROVERBS 12:18 NASB

CONTEMPLATE:

- Why do words have such potential to harm people?

- How do words bring healing?

APPLY:

Sometimes ancient figurative language lines up neatly with our own. In the scriptures, the words *tongue* or *mouth* mean speech or language, like we would say, his "native tongue" or "a foul mouth." Figurative language is a powerful way to communicate and was used often throughout the book of Proverbs.

There's an old children's ditty that goes: "Sticks and stones may break my bones, but words will never hurt me." It makes a good retort on the playground when you're six, but it's not always true. We've all felt the stab of hurtful words, and we're all guilty of wounding someone else. Taming the tongue is an ongoing challenge. James wrote, "With the tongue we praise our Lord and Father, and with it we curse human beings, who have been made in God's likeness. Out of the same mouth come praise and cursing. My brothers and sisters, this should not be" (James 3:9–10 NIV).

Since we know that "out of the abundance of the heart the mouth speaks" (Matthew 12:34 ESV), we have to start with our inner man, meditating on the Word, with praise and thanksgiving. Only by filling our hearts with God will we have a chance to bring healing words and follow Paul's instruction: "Do not let any unwholesome talk come out of your mouths, but only what is helpful for building others up according to their needs, that it may benefit those who listen" (Ephesians 4:29 NIV).

Words are powerful and the wise man will use them to bring healing.

PRAY:

Lord, You spoke the heavens and earth into existence; teach me to speak healing to those who need it.

THE WICKED

Read Proverbs 23:17–35

KEY VERSES:

*Do not let your heart envy sinners, but live in the
fear of the LORD always. Certainly there is a future,
and your hope will not be cut off. Listen, my son,
and be wise, and direct your heart in the way.*

PROVERBS 23:17–19 NASB

CONTEMPLATE:

- What is there to envy about the wicked?

- What are believers to set their hearts on?

- What is the promise for those who live in "the
fear of the LORD"?

APPLY:

Sometimes studying the Bible means rethinking
the meanings of words we assume we know. Today's
proverb offers us that opportunity.

We don't use the word *sinner* much, and even
in religious settings, it's often used in a generic way
like, "Jesus came to save sinners." Of course, we
"all have sinned and fall short of the glory of God"
(Romans 3:23 NASB), but that's not really what the
term denotes in the scriptures. The biblical usage

of *sinner* refers not to merely imperfect or flawed people but to the ungodly who embrace rebellion as a lifestyle.

And sometimes sinners are very successful people! Frankly, it can be discouraging, as the psalmist confessed: "Truly God is good to Israel, to those whose hearts are pure. But as for me, I almost lost my footing. My feet were slipping, and I was almost gone. For I envied the proud when I saw them prosper despite their wickedness" (Psalm 73:1–3 NLT). Thankfully, Asaph stuck to the path of wisdom, regained hope, and saw the future that today's reading promises. "You guide me with your counsel, and afterward you will take me into glory. Whom have I in heaven but you? And earth has nothing I desire besides you" (Psalm 73:24–25 NIV).

Nothing sinners gain on earth can compare to what awaits the faithful.

PRAY:

Gracious Lord, keep my heart from envying those who reject You. May my hope rest solely on Christ.

FATHERS AND MENTORS

Read Proverbs 4

KEY VERSES:

Listen, my sons, to the instruction of a father, and pay attention so that you may gain understanding, for I give you good teaching; do not abandon my instruction. When I was a son to my father, tender and the only son in the sight of my mother, he taught me and said to me, "Let your heart take hold of my words; keep my commandments and live; acquire wisdom! Acquire understanding!"

PROVERBS 4:1–5 NASB

CONTEMPLATE:

- Who is responsible for passing wisdom to the next generation?

- Why is an older man's teaching so important?

APPLY:

Fatherhood can be a complicated subject. Some of us have (or had) highly engaged dads, some absent dads, and some no dads. No matter your situation, today's proverb speaks to all men—even if you're not a father.

God doesn't expect fathers to pass along all wisdom to their children, but each father can pass along the love of wisdom. No man has all the answers, but each man is responsible to equip the next generation to embrace the wisdom of a godly life; to mentor as God gives him the chance.

We all need mentors in addition to our own fathers or, if necessary, in place of them. And each of us can become a mentor. Paul referred to both Timothy and Titus as his "sons in the faith" (1 Timothy 1:2, Titus 1:4), and he dealt with his congregations "as a father deals with his own children, encouraging, comforting and urging you to live lives worthy of God" (1 Thessalonians 2:11–12 NIV). Paul's mentoring covered four generations: "what you have heard from me in the presence of many witnesses entrust to faithful men, who will be able to teach others also" (2 Timothy 2:2 ESV).

All men can embrace the role of mentor whether they have children or not.

PRAY:
Perfect Father, grant me the ability to pass wisdom on to the next generation.

THE NEXT GENERATION

Read Proverbs 22:1–16

KEY VERSE:

Train up a child in the way he should go;
even when he is old he will not depart from it.
PROVERBS 22:6 ESV

CONTEMPLATE:

- What does it mean to "train up a child"?

- Does this verse promise that all godly parents
  will produce godly children?

APPLY:

It is God's design that we grow and mature. In His
wisdom, He created a process—a journey—integral
to the human experience. Even Jesus, though God in
the flesh, "grew in wisdom and stature, and in favor
with God and man" (Luke 2:52 NIV).

The Hebrew word for "train up" (*chanak*) occurs
five times in the Bible, normally translated as "dedicate" (referring to houses or Solomon's temple). That
adds an interesting take on today's verse. Parents are
to dedicate, or *offer up*, their children to the Lord by
giving them the right start on their journey. Of course,
it's not a guarantee of a righteous life since each man
makes his own choices, but those who do follow "in

the way he *should* go" will always look back gratefully to the training they received as a child.

That training process isn't always easy. Sometimes we have to exercise tough love. "Folly is bound up in the heart of a child, but the rod of discipline will drive it far away" (Proverbs 22:15 niv). The scriptures do not advocate abuse, but they clearly teach that disciplining a child is better than allowing him to get his own way. The same is true for us as God's children. "Endure hardship as discipline; God is treating you as his children. For what children are not disciplined by their father? If you are not disciplined—and everyone undergoes discipline— then you are not legitimate, not true sons and daughters at all" (Hebrews 12:7–8 niv).

PRAY:

Good Father, help me to raise up the next generation in wisdom and to accept Your discipline as a child myself.

LIKE FAMILY

Read 1 Timothy 5:1–16

Key Verses:

Never speak harshly to an older man, but appeal to him respectfully as you would to your own father. Talk to younger men as you would to your own brothers. Treat older women as you would your mother, and treat younger women with all purity as you would your own sisters.
1 Timothy 5:1–2 NLT

Contemplate:

- How should a man relate to other men, both older and younger?

- How are older women to be treated?

- What additional instruction applies to young women?

Apply:

The scriptures record all manner of dysfunctional families from Cain who murdered his brother, Abel, out of jealousy, to Noah who cursed one of his sons, to Joseph who was sold into slavery by his brothers, to David whose son Absalom tried to usurp the throne. But despite the failings of any particular family, the family was God's design to fill the earth, and through His Son to redeem it as he promised Abraham: "in you and your offspring [Jesus] shall all the families of the earth be blessed" (Genesis 28:14 ESV).

Family was also the Father's design for the church to follow. Paul said, "I write so that you will know how one should act in the household of God" (1 Timothy 3:15 NASB). Paul even tied an elder's qualification to his own family's experience: "For if a man cannot manage his own household, how can he take care of God's church?" (1 Timothy 3:5 NLT).

To act wisely, we need to envision a healthy family dynamic, not treating older men disrespectfully, encouraging younger men as brothers, serving older women like our own mothers, and behaving toward younger women as sisters, without any hint of impropriety. In other words, "In your relationships with one another, have the same mindset as Christ Jesus" (Philippians 2:5 NIV).

PRAY:

Perfect Father, give me wisdom toward those I serve so I may be useful in Your household.

WORK, PART 1

Read Proverbs 24:30–34

KEY VERSES:

I passed by the field of a sluggard, by the vineyard of a man lacking sense, and behold, it was all overgrown with thorns; the ground was covered with nettles, and its stone wall was broken down.

PROVERBS 24:30–31 ESV

CONTEMPLATE:

- What is the result of laziness and neglect?
- What lesson does the writer draw from his observations?

APPLY:

Work is foundational to all existence. It only turned into labor after man sinned. Part of the consequences of the fall specifically included "cursed is the ground because of you; in pain you shall eat of it all the days of your life; thorns and thistles it shall bring forth for you; and you shall eat the plants of the field" (Genesis 3:17–18 ESV). The satisfying days of the garden were gone; from now on the world would push back on man's efforts.

There's a funny meme that captures the grind that work can be: the first five days after the weekend are always the hardest. But the consequences of "a little sleep, a little slumber, a little folding of the hands to rest" (Proverbs 24:33 NIV) can be disastrous. The man "lacking sense" had a vineyard—a God-given opportunity—that he squandered. Like one of the men in the parable Jesus told of a master who gave three servants a sum of money to invest "each according to his own ability" (Matthew 25:15 NASB). Two worked to produce a return by investing, but the third buried the money and took no risks—even though that was the entire point of being entrusted with the money. The master pronounced the first two "good and faithful" and the third "wicked" and "lazy" (Matthew 25:23, 26 NIV).

The wise man sees the opportunity to work as a blessing but also a responsibility.

PRAY:

Lord, strengthen me to take responsibility and be more intentional in all the work You've assigned me.

WORK, PART 2

Read Proverbs 6:6–11

KEY VERSES:

Go to the ant, you sluggard; consider its ways and be wise! It has no commander, no overseer or ruler, yet it stores its provisions in summer and gathers its food at harvest.
PROVERBS 6:6–8 NIV

CONTEMPLATE:

- What characteristics does the ant display that serves as an example of wisdom?

- Who tells the ant what to do and when?

APPLY:

In yesterday's study we saw how work became labor after the fall, and that man was destined to face opposition to his efforts ever after. Work would still be a part of the man's identity, but its increased difficulty would present the temptation to avoid responsibility, to become lax, to become a sluggard. So, Solomon directs our attention to the lowly ant.

The ant is "wise" because it needs no one to cause it to take responsibility—it's a self-starter! The ant looks ahead and makes plans. Like the ant, the wise make no excuses to provide for themselves and their family. Whether you're in a profession, a career, a trade, or still trying to find the right job, wisdom tells us to look to the ant for the basic lesson about taking responsibility.

The workplace isn't the only arena where men can grow slack. Family, church, and community all require taking responsibility. Marriages do not thrive without effort, and children do not develop without care and energy, and a congregation falters without those who serve diligently. Is taking responsibility and being intentional easy? Of course not! But through the Holy Spirit we are to, "Work willingly at whatever you do, as though you were working for the Lord rather than for people" (Colossians 3:23 NLT).

PRAY:

Gracious Father, may the work of my hands be a testimony of my faith in You.

GOD'S ECONOMY

Read Proverbs 11:23–28

KEY VERSES:

One person gives freely, yet gains even more; another withholds unduly, but comes to poverty. A generous person will prosper; whoever refreshes others will be refreshed.

PROVERBS 11:24–25 NIV

CONTEMPLATE:

- What principles of generosity do you see in today's reading?

- What seems contradictory about this approach to wealth?

APPLY:

It's not surprising that the way the world sees things is often at odds with heaven. Perhaps no subject more clearly demonstrates that than money. Jesus pointedly said, "No one can serve two masters. . . . You cannot serve both God and money" (Matthew 6:24 NIV).

Today's verse is about living contrary to the world's approach to wealth and its purpose. The world says, store up all the wealth you can and use it for your own satisfaction. But God's path leads to being open handed in faith, knowing where wealth comes from to begin with.

Moses warned the people, who because of their enslavement in Egypt had never owned land for themselves, "Beware lest you say in your heart, 'My power and the might of my hand have gotten me this wealth.' You shall remember the LORD your God, for it is he who gives you power to get wealth" (Deuteronomy 8:17–18 ESV). From the Bible's perspective, you and I have never gotten a paycheck that wasn't a gift from God.

When King David collected money for his son Solomon to build God's temple, everyone gave "freely and wholeheartedly to the LORD" (1 Chronicles 29:9 NIV). But the king didn't take credit for such generosity: "But who am I, and who are my people, that we should be able to give as generously as this? Everything comes from you, and we have given you only what comes from your hand" (1 Chronicles 29:14 NIV). Really, you can only ever give back to God.

PRAY:

Generous Father, show me how to give more and more, trusting You to supply all my needs.

THE POOR

Read Proverbs 19:16–18

KEY VERSE:
Whoever is kind to the poor lends to the LORD,
and he will reward them for what they have done.
PROVERBS 19:17 NIV

CONTEMPLATE:

- Why would God consider kindness to the poor as a "loan" to Himself?

- Who are the poor today?

- What is promised to those who are kind to the poor?

APPLY:

In the scriptures, the Lord consistently aligns Himself with the underdog: the widow, the orphan, and the poor. "I know that the LORD secures justice for the poor and upholds the cause of the needy" (Psalm 140:12 NIV). "A father to the fatherless, a defender of widows, is God in his holy dwelling" (Psalm 68:5 NIV). His concern for those who are the lowest is part of His pattern of revealing Himself to the humble and shaming the proud. As we studied earlier, "God chose things despised by the world, things counted as nothing at all, and used them to bring to nothing what the world considers important" (1 Corinthians 1:28 NLT).

The "poor" are those whose lot in life is one of weakness and vulnerability—a group to be helped, not ignored or used. But there's another kind of "poor" we need to be discerning about—the sluggard. God gave many laws to protect the poor, but to the slacker He gave only warnings: "A slack hand causes poverty" (Proverbs 10:4 ESV); "mere talk tends only to poverty" (Proverbs 14:23 ESV); "Love not sleep, lest you come to poverty" (Proverbs 20:13 ESV). The sluggard needs to face the consequences of his choices as Paul, who loved "the poor," commanded: "if anyone is not willing to work, then he is not to eat, either" (2 Thessalonians 3:10 NASB). We are called to be generous to the poor, not support the lazy.

PRAY:

Father, give me a tender heart to the poor and a discerning heart toward those who need a different kind of help.

THE UNCERTAINTY
OF RICHES

Read Proverbs 18:10–12

KEY VERSES:
The name of the LORD is a strong tower;
the righteous man runs into it and is safe.
A rich man's wealth is his strong city, and
like a high wall in his imagination.
PROVERBS 18:10–11 ESV

CONTEMPLATE:

- Where do the righteous take refuge?

- What is the mistake of the "rich man"?

- What is the point of wealth?

APPLY:

In yesterday's study, we saw that the Lord is sympathetic to the poor and the vulnerable. Conversely, He has abundant warnings for "the rich" who trust in money rather than the Lord since riches remain here. "For when they die, they take nothing with them. Their wealth will not follow them into the grave" (Psalm 49:17 NLT).

The lure of riches can be exhausting. "Do not weary yourself to gain wealth; stop dwelling on it.

When you set your eyes on it, it is gone" (Proverbs 23:4–5 NASB). Money can quickly disappear! And even if our wealth doesn't leave us, *we* might leave it—as Jesus pointed out in the parable of a rich man who presumed upon the future:

> *And I'll sit back and say to myself, "My friend, you have enough stored away for years to come. Now take it easy! Eat, drink, and be merry!" "But God said to him, 'You fool! You will die this very night. Then who will get everything you worked for?' "Yes, a person is a fool to store up earthly wealth but not have a rich relationship with God."*
> *Luke 12:19–21 NLT*

There's nothing inherently wrong with wealth as long as we heed Paul's command: "Instruct those who are rich in this present world not to be conceited or to set their hope on the uncertainty of riches, but on God, who richly supplies us with all things to enjoy" (1 Timothy 6:17 NASB).

PRAY:

Your name, O Lord, is my sanctuary and my sufficiency; keep me from trusting in the wealth of this world.

SOWING AND REAPING

Read Proverbs 3:7–12

KEY VERSE:

Honor the LORD with your wealth, with the firstfruits of all your crops; then your barns will be filled to overflowing, and your vats will brim over with new wine.
PROVERBS 3:9–10 NIV

CONTEMPLATE:

- How do we honor the Lord with our wealth?

- What are "firstfruits"?

- What happens to the one who puts God first in his financial practices?

APPLY:

As you know, proverbs do not provide rigid formulas; they highlight principles. What they underscore should be considered in light of the full teaching of the Bible. Today's proverb isn't a guarantee of increasing one's bank account; it's about putting the Lord first in our finances and trusting Him to take care of us in a cycle He designed known as *sowing and reaping*. He provides, we invest, and we gain a return so we can reinvest.

When the Corinthian church was preparing a donation for the needy in Jerusalem, Paul said, "Remember this: Whoever sows sparingly will also reap sparingly, and whoever sows generously will also reap generously" (2 Corinthians 9:6 NIV). Paul echoes Solomon's observation that, "A generous person will prosper; whoever refreshes others will be refreshed" (Proverbs 11:25 NIV). The *reaping* or *refreshing* we receive may or may not be financial, though it could be. Paul didn't readily distinguish between material and spiritual blessings since, in either case, the point was to reinvest. Paul was perfectly confident that "he who supplies seed to the sower and bread for food will also supply and increase your store of seed and will enlarge the harvest of your righteousness" (2 Corinthians 9:10 NIV), so the cycle of blessing others would continue.

And happily, giving isn't about the amount, "For if the willingness is there, the gift is acceptable according to what one has, not according to what one does not have" (2 Corinthians 8:12 NIV). We can all participate!

PRAY:

Giver of all things, may I always put You first in my finances, trusting You to provide.

DEBT

Read Proverbs 22:7–9

KEY VERSE:

The rich rules over the poor, and the
borrower is the slave of the lender.
PROVERBS 22:7 ESV

CONTEMPLATE:

- How does debt equate to "slavery"?

- Is borrowing money something the Bible
  frowns upon?

- Is it even possible to live in a modern world
  without debt?

APPLY:

Often the sayings of the wise are formulated as simple
observations—*A penny saved is a penny earned*—rather
than directives—*Don't take any wooden nickels*. Today's
verse is just such an observation. It functions as a road
sign warning of what's ahead. How you utilize that
information is up to you.

In the Old Testament, lending was not forbidden
but charging interest of fellow Israelites was. "Do not
charge a fellow Israelite interest, whether on money
or food or anything else that may earn interest. You

may charge a foreigner interest, but not a fellow Israelite" (Deuteronomy 23:19–20 NIV). If there's a lender, there must be a borrower.

While the Bible does not forbid debt, it certainly doesn't encourage it. Debt may not mean literal slavery these days but it's a form of obligation that can interfere with our legitimate obligations to God. Therefore, debt shouldn't be entered into lightly or, to be very specific, with thoughts of not repaying. "The wicked borrow and do not repay" (Psalm 37:21 NIV). Paul commanded us, "Give to everyone what you owe them: If you owe taxes, pay taxes; if revenue, then revenue; if respect, then respect; if honor, then honor. Let no debt remain outstanding" (Romans 13:7–8 NIV).

Today, the easiest way to get in over your head is through credit cards. The wise will handle them with extreme caution or—better yet—not at all! Enter contract purchases like houses and cars remembering today's verse. While theoretically they could be sold to repay an outstanding balance, they still involve risk.

PRAY:
*O Lord, keep me from enslaving myself
for things that do not last!*

AMBITION

Read Proverbs 25:1–10

KEY VERSES:

*Do not exalt yourself in the king's presence,
and do not claim a place among his great men;
it is better for him to say to you, "Come up here,"
than for him to humiliate you before his nobles.*
PROVERBS 25:6–7 NIV

CONTEMPLATE:

- What situation in your life would equate to being "in the king's presence"?

- What does this verse say happens to the man who attempts to exalt himself?

APPLY:

Like all Hebrew men, Jesus was educated in the scriptures. He quoted the scriptures extensively, weaving them into His own teachings with fresh authority. The *most* educated men in Israel—the Pharisees—often missed how the scriptures applied to themselves. One Sabbath, Jesus had been invited "to eat in the house of a *prominent* Pharisee" (Luke 14:1 NIV). There He took the opportunity to deftly apply the principle of today's proverb by changing the context from a king's table to a common wedding feast:

*When he noticed how the guests picked the places
of honor at the table, he told them this parable:
"When someone invites you to a wedding feast,
do not take the place of honor, for a person
more distinguished than you may have been
invited. If so, the host who invited both of you
will come and say to you, 'Give this person
your seat.' Then, humiliated, you will have to
take the least important place. But when you
are invited, take the lowest place, so that when
your host comes, he will say to you, 'Friend,
move up to a better place.' Then you will be
honored in the presence of all the other guests.*
Luke 14:7–10 NIV

Wisdom tells us not to exalt ourselves since
"God chose the foolish things of the world to shame
the wise" (1 Corinthians 1:27 NIV). Better to count
yourself among the lowly and let Him lift you up as
He sees fit.

PRAY:

*You alone, O King, exalt and bless.
I simply rejoice in being at Your table.*

THE TEST OF PRAISE

Read Proverbs 27:17–22

KEY VERSE:

The crucible is for silver and the furnace for gold,
and each is tested by the praise accorded him.
PROVERBS 27:21 NASB

CONTEMPLATE:

- What is the point of a crucible in refining silver or a furnace for gold?

- How do praise and honor test a man?

APPLY:

Most of us would probably think of testing as hardship, affliction, or persecution. Those certainly do test what we are made of the way a crucible shows the quality of a metal by bringing the dross to the surface. But there's a more subtle test of our inner qualities.

Take the example of Herod Agrippa, the Roman-raised grandson of Herod the Great (the king when Jesus was born) who ruled after his uncle Herod Antipas (the king during Jesus' life). Herod Agrippa was overseeing a political event, surrounded by people begging for his help, when his time of testing came: "On an appointed day Herod put on his royal robes, took his seat upon the throne, and delivered an oration to them. And the people were shouting, 'The voice of a god, and not of a man!' Immediately an angel of the Lord struck him down, because he did not give God the glory, and he was eaten by worms and breathed his last" (Acts 12:21–23 ESV).

Herod, a Jew by birth, allowed himself to be praised as a god (apparently Roman thinking had rubbed off) and paid a heavy price. Conversely, when the pagans of Lystra attempted to sacrifice offerings to Paul and Barnabas for healing a crippled man in Acts 14, the apostles "tore their garments" and rushed into the crowd to stop them. They are examples to us that we can pass the test of success too because "a person with a changed heart seeks praise from God, not from people" (Romans 2:29 NLT).

PRAY:
Guard me, O God, from the temptation
to seek the useless praise of this world.

CORRECTION

Read Proverbs 15:30–32

KEY VERSE:
Whoever heeds life-giving correction
will be at home among the wise.
PROVERBS 15:31 NIV

CONTEMPLATE:

- Why is correction so hard to take?

- Does it matter where correction comes from?

- What does it feel like to offer correction to another?

APPLY:

One of the themes repeated in wisdom literature is humility and the critical need to heed correction for our own benefit.

Maturity is voluntary; we don't have to change. Man is allowed to remain ignorant and face the consequences. "Whoever ignores instruction despises himself, but he who listens to reproof gains intelligence" (Proverbs 15:32 ESV).

King David has one of the most famous stories of correction and redemption in the Bible. After hiding his adultery and subsequent pregnancy of Bathsheba by setting up her husband to be killed in a military campaign, the king openly took her as a wife without any hint of remorse. This was the same David who as a young man was chosen by God to be king and described by God as "a man after my heart, who will do all my will" (Acts 13:22 ESV). When rebuked by Nathan the prophet, David responded in repentance (2 Samuel 12, Psalm 51).

Being corrected isn't pleasant, but correcting others can be just as hard. Nathan could have been punished for speaking the truth to a king as John the Baptist was by the adulterous King Herod (Matthew 14:3–4). You can tell a lot about a man's character from his reaction to rebuke. "Do not reprove a scoffer, or he will hate you; reprove a wise man, and he will love you" (Proverbs 9:8 ESV). Whether we are corrected gently by a friend or harshly by an adversary, we should bear in mind that, "A rebuke goes deeper into a man of understanding than a hundred blows into a fool" (Proverbs 17:10 ESV).

PRAY:
Correct me often, O God, in any way that helps me become more like Christ.

HONOR

Read Proverbs 15:32–33 & Daniel 2

KEY VERSE:

Wisdom's instruction is to fear the LORD,
and humility comes before honor.
PROVERBS 15:33 NIV

CONTEMPLATE:

- What does it look like to be honored by the Lord?

- What is the prerequisite for being honored by the Father?

APPLY:

One way of allowing scripture to explain scripture is by finding a story that demonstrates the idea of a particular verse.

About 200 years after civil war divided the Jews, Israel fell to the Assyrians, and eventually Judah fell to the Babylonians who took captives "of the nobility, youths without blemish, of good appearance and skillful in all wisdom, endowed with knowledge, understanding learning, and competent to stand in the king's palace" (Daniel 1:3–4 ESV), including Daniel and three friends. Even in captivity they feared the Lord and refused unclean foods according to Jewish law. God so blessed them that, "in every matter of wisdom and understanding about which the king inquired of them, he found them ten times better than all the magicians and enchanters that were in all his kingdom" (Daniel 1:20 ESV).

A year later King Nebuchadnezzar had a disturbing dream. Not trusting his wise men, he demanded, "tell me the dream, and then I'll know that you can tell me what it means" (Daniel 2:9 NLT). Infuriated by their inability to describe the dream, the king commanded the death of all the wise men in Babylon! But Daniel, in a last-minute audience with Nebuchadnezzar, saved the lives of hundreds by revealing both the dream and its interpretation. Daniel could have taken credit but rather made it clear, "it is not because I am wiser than anyone else that I know the secret of your dream, but because God wants you to understand" (Daniel 2:30 NLT).

The king was ecstatic, honoring both Daniel *and* his God.

PRAY:

Wise Father, may I always fear You so I can make You known in this generation.

BOUNDARIES

Read Proverbs 23:9–11

KEY VERSE:

Do not move an ancient boundary stone or encroach on the fields of the fatherless.
PROVERBS 23:10 NIV

CONTEMPLATE:

- What were boundary stones used for in ancient times?

- What reason would anyone have to move one?

- Is there a modern equivalent to boundary stones?

APPLY:

For almost as long as humans have owned land, they've had to mark the boundaries. Historical markers exist all across the world, from Egypt to Ireland and from China to Greece.

The people of Israel did not know what it was like to occupy their own land for over 440 years. So, naturally, there needed to be rules set up to avoid conflicts between neighbors. The boundary stone represented ownership; but more than that, it ensured stability for the entire society, generation after generation. "Do not move your neighbor's boundary stone set up by your predecessors in the inheritance you receive in the land the LORD your God is giving you to possess" (Deuteronomy 19:14 NIV). Moving a boundary stone equated to the theft of land assigned to each family by God Himself; most often it meant the oppression of the weak by the strong.

As physical boundary stones existed to create stability from one generation to the next, so there are faith boundaries set up for our stability that have been passed down to us: the divinity of Christ and His substitutionary death that allows for salvation; the call to repentance and a holy life by the power of the Spirit; participation in the body of Christ and bearing witness to the world of Jesus; the authority of all scripture. These are among the "boundary stones" that must not be moved or else we risk robbing the faith from the next generation.

PRAY:

Good Father, You have made Yourself known from generation to generation through Your Word. Teach me to handle the truth in a way that safeguards the next generation of believers.

UNDERSTANDING ECCLESIASTES

Read Ecclesiastes 1

KEY VERSES:

I, the Teacher, was king over Israel in Jerusalem. I applied my mind to study and to explore by wisdom all that is done under the heavens. What a heavy burden God has laid on mankind! I have seen all the things that are done under the sun; all of them are meaningless, a chasing after the wind.

ECCLESIASTES 1:12–14 NIV

CONTEMPLATE:

- Who is this Teacher that was also king over Israel?

- How would you describe his tone in this personal introduction?

APPLY:

As we discussed previously, Ecclesiastes is part of the wisdom literature of the scripture and must be approached uniquely. Unlike the book of Proverbs with its memorable sayings, Ecclesiastes must be taken in its entirety like a memoir that unfolds chapter by chapter, only complete at the end.

"The words of the Teacher, son of David, king in Jerusalem" (Ecclesiastes 1:1 NIV) tells us that this is Solomon's work. His breadth of understanding was unparalleled; as was his wealth, power, and reputation. If anyone had the opportunity to explore "all that is done under the heavens" it was Solomon. He undertook great projects—homes, gardens, vineyards, and reservoirs; he amassed great wealth, herds, flocks, male and female slaves (Ecclesiastes 2:4-8); and "had 700 wives of royal birth and 300 concubines" (1 Kings 11:3 NLT). And as we've seen, that did not help his spiritual life at all!

As Solomon himself put it: "I denied myself nothing my eyes desired; I refused my heart no pleasure" (Ecclesiastes 2:10 NIV). Sounds like a dream, but for Solomon it was all "chasing after the wind"—a disappointing cycle of toil "under the heavens." Solomon learned how burdensome and unfair life can be. You might say the tone of Ecclesiastes is world weary— but not without hope, as we'll see in further studies.

PRAY:

Thank You, O Lord, that I don't have to test this life to know You are my only hope.

LISTENING

Read Ecclesiastes 5:1–7

KEY VERSES:

*Guard your steps when you go to the house of
God. To draw near to listen is better than to
offer the sacrifice of fools, for they do not know
that they are doing evil. Be not rash with your
mouth, nor let your heart be hasty to utter a
word before God, for God is in heaven and you
are on earth. Therefore let your words be few.*
ECCLESIASTES 5:1–2 ESV

CONTEMPLATE:

- Why would a sacrifice to God ever be foolish?
- How should we approach the Almighty?

APPLY:

The temple Solomon built was referred to as the
"house of God" (*bethel*). Of course, no one thought the
Almighty was *only* in the temple because as today's
verse notes, "God is in heaven." Solomon emphasized
this during the temple's dedication: "But will God
really dwell on earth with humans? The heavens, even
the highest heavens, cannot contain you. How much
less this temple I have built!" (2 Chronicles 6:18 NIV).
But the Living God did intend to use the temple in

a unique way. "I have chosen and consecrated this temple so that my Name may be there forever. My eyes and my heart will always be there" (2 Chronicles 7:16 NIV). Only fools would treat that lightly!

It was wise to seek out God and listen to Him since He intentionally placed Himself within reach. As the psalmist declared, "Now that you have made me listen, I finally understand—you don't require burnt offerings or sin offerings" (Psalm 40:6 NLT). The fool believes he can "game the system" with sacrifices that pay for his sin and allow him to go about his way. And even sincere people should pause—God doesn't need rash promises or excuses any more than burnt offerings. He needs (if you can say God needs anything) us to listen.

PRAY:
Sovereign Lord, put a guard over my mouth and teach me to listen.

GREED

Read Ecclesiastes 5:8–17

KEY VERSES:

*Whoever loves money never has enough; whoever
loves wealth is never satisfied with their income.
This too is meaningless. As goods increase, so do
those who consume them. And what benefit are they
to the owners except to feast their eyes on them?*
ECCLESIASTES 5:10–11 NIV

CONTEMPLATE:

- How does Solomon, who was wealthy beyond imagination, view the love of money?

- What does wealth truly accomplish for its owner?

APPLY:

We know Ecclesiastes has a world-weary tone, but in today's verses, Solomon sounds downright cynical! And with good reason—his own experience. Not only was his personal wealth vast but he "made silver as common as stones in Jerusalem" (1 Kings 10:27 NASB). As he and his people grew wealthy, he witnessed firsthand the seduction of riches.

We've already seen that riches are not to be trusted. Wealth can fly away, or we can leave it all behind when we die. Still, its allure remains strong. Solomon experienced the disappointment of accumulating wealth. It never truly satisfies, so enough is never enough. Hundreds of years later, Socrates echoed Solomon's observation: "He who is not contented with what he has, would not be contented with what he would like to have."

Jesus made this stark contrast: "No one can serve two masters. . . .You cannot serve God and wealth" (Matthew 6:24 NASB). Paul expanded on His thought: "But those who want to get rich fall into temptation and a trap, and many foolish and harmful desires which plunge people into ruin and destruction. For the love of money is a root of all sorts of evil, and some by longing for it have wandered away from the faith and pierced themselves with many griefs" (1 Timothy 6:9–10 NASB).

Considering what the "love of money" can cost us, wealth can just be too expensive!

PRAY:
Father, You are the source of all things, and in Your Son, I have been made wealthy beyond measure.

CONTENTMENT

Read Ecclesiastes 5:18–20

KEY VERSE:

*Moreover, when God gives someone wealth
and possessions, and the ability to enjoy
them, to accept their lot and be happy
in their toil—this is a gift of God.*
ECCLESIASTES 5:19 NIV

CONTEMPLATE:

- Where does contentment come from?

- Why is contentment a gift from God?

- What does accepting your "lot" in life mean?

APPLY:

There are two men we all know: the one who makes a lot of money but never seems happy and the one who makes a modest living but can't wait to go to work every day. Most of us probably fall somewhere in between.

No matter how much talent and education and opportunity we have, we face limits. Wealth and success are great but in and of themselves offer no guarantee of fulfillment. There will always be something beyond our reach—limits that comprise our "lot" in life. Sometimes these limits—especially financial—can tempt us to discontentment. Not the kind that motivates a career change or going back to school but the kind that results in coveting, complaining, and ingratitude. And let's face it, contentment can be elusive in a society that leverages discontentment to sell us things—for a price, we can find satisfaction. Solomon pointed out the irony of this: contentment can't be bought because it's a *gift*. "A person can do nothing better than to eat and drink and find satisfaction in their own toil. This too, I see, *is from the hand of God*, for without him, who can eat or find enjoyment?" (Ecclesiastes 2:24–25 NIV).

The treadmill of discontentment stops when we accept that God Himself is our lot. "Keep your life free from love of money, and be content with what you have, for he has said, 'I will never leave you nor forsake you'" (Hebrews 13:5 ESV).

He is more than enough.

PRAY:

Gracious and generous God, You alone are my satisfaction; teach me to wait upon You.

PARTNERSHIP

Read Ecclesiastes 4:9–12

KEY VERSES:

Two are better than one, because they have a
good return for their labor: if either of them falls
down, one can help the other up. But pity anyone
who falls and has no one to help them up.
ECCLESIASTES 4:9–10 NIV

CONTEMPLATE:

- Why are two better than one?

- What happens to the person who has no one else to rely on?

- In what areas of your life do feel you don't have someone to "help you up"?

APPLY:

Today's reading may be familiar since it's used frequently in weddings. While this verse isn't about marriage, it certainly does apply because man was designed for companionship and partnership. "It is not good for the man to be alone; I will make him a helper suitable for him" (Genesis 2:18 NASB). The Hebrew word translated as "suitable" literally means "corresponding to." That is, a partner equal and adequate to himself.

But marriage isn't the only partnership ordained by God for our well-being. "A friend loves at all times, and a brother is born for adversity" (Proverbs 17:17 ESV). Even married men need other men because "iron sharpens iron, and one man sharpens another" (Proverbs 27:17 ESV). Frankly, sometimes that can be uncomfortable. If we fall spiritually, help might be in the form of rebuke. Hopefully we remember that "Faithful are the wounds of a friend" (Proverbs 27:6 ESV). If we find ourselves being the one offering that kind of help, Paul had this advice: "Brothers, if anyone is caught in any transgression, you who are spiritual should restore him in a spirit of gentleness. . . . Bear one another's burdens, and so fulfill the law of Christ" (Galatians 6:1–2 ESV).

We were never meant to go through this life isolated from fellowship. We need to forge deep partnerships with those who want a good return on their spiritual journey as well.

PRAY:

*God of all comfort, help me to become a good
partner to many in Your kingdom.*

GOD'S SOVEREIGNTY

Read Ecclesiastes 7:10–14

KEY VERSES:

Do not say, "Why is it that the former days were better than these?" For it is not from wisdom that you ask about this. . . . On the day of prosperity be happy, but on the day of adversity consider: God has made the one as well as the other.

ECCLESIASTES 7:10,14 NASB

CONTEMPLATE:

- What can be unwise about remembering the "good old days"?

- Where do good times and bad times both come from?

APPLY:

Most of us have some memories we could refer to as the "good old days," and there's nothing wrong with looking back with fondness. Solomon's point in today's reading is not that we should forget the past but that we're not to complain about today.

Solomon's famous saying that "there is nothing new under the sun" (Ecclesiastes 1:9 NIV) was not about technology or culture but the human experience. Prosperity and adversity come to us all. And yet, somehow, they *both* proceed from a loving God—meaning lamenting the present and glorifying the past is a form of accusation against the Almighty.

Job had a grip on this, at least in the beginning. When his wife suggested he curse God and die to escape his suffering, he rebuked her. "You are speaking as one of the foolish women speaks. Shall we actually accept good from God but not accept adversity?" (Job 2:10 NASB). The prophet Isaiah addressed the real problem—the question of who is most qualified to be in charge: "Does a clay pot argue with its maker? Does the clay dispute with the one who shapes it, saying, 'Stop, you're doing it wrong!' Does the pot exclaim, 'How clumsy can you be?'" (Isaiah 45:9 NLT).

To continue in wisdom, we must all settle Paul's question: "Does the potter not have a right over the clay?" (Romans 9:21 NASB).

PRAY:

Sovereign King, help me to embrace You every day in all circumstances with thanksgiving.

SOLOMON'S CONCLUSION

Read Ecclesiastes 12

KEY VERSES:
The end of the matter; all has been heard.
Fear God and keep his commandments,
for this is the whole duty of man. For God
will bring every deed into judgment, with
every secret thing, whether good or evil.
ECCLESIASTES 12:13–14 ESV

CONTEMPLATE:

- What were the final two pieces of advice
  Solomon had for his readers?

- What reasons does he give for his conclusion?

APPLY:

Solomon was allowed to explore all life's possibilities while still retaining the gift of wisdom. That gift allowed him to see through every false promise this world makes apart from the Creator. As he grew older, however, he found the gift burdensome: "For in much wisdom is much vexation, and he who increases knowledge increases sorrow" (Ecclesiastes 1:18 ESV). But in God's mercy, vexation drove Solomon to the correct conclusion.

If "the fear of the LORD is the beginning of wisdom" (Proverbs 9:10 ESV), then the result of wisdom is obedience to God's commandments—not as a means to earn salvation but to know and experience God. The common translation of Ecclesiastes 12:13, "the whole *duty* of man," is literally "the whole man." Fearing and obeying God is more than a responsibility; it's meant to be part of our identity. We do not exist without God, and seeking any satisfaction without Him will only end in frustration as Solomon learned.

Solomon, as we've seen, clearly ignored significant parts of the scriptures. But by the end of his life's journey, King David's son had come full circle, agreeing with what had been written hundreds of years earlier: "Serve only the LORD your God and fear him alone. Obey his commands, listen to his voice, and cling to him" (Deuteronomy 13:4 NLT). After all his experiences, wealth, and wisdom, Solomon ended up back at square one!

PRAY:

Father, help me to fear You. May I never take the sacrifice of Your Son for granted.

SAMSON'S FOLLY

Read Judges 16

KEY VERSES:

[Delilah] said to him, "How can you say, 'I love you,' when you won't confide in me? This is the third time you have made a fool of me and haven't told me the secret of your great strength." With such nagging she prodded him day after day until he was sick to death of it. So he told her everything.
JUDGES 16:15–17 NIV

CONTEMPLATE:

- What was Samson famous for?

- What did Delilah accuse Samson of?

- Why did Samson eventually give in?

APPLY:

Samson had a great start. An angel promised his barren mother, "You will become pregnant and have a son whose head is never to be touched by a razor because the boy is to be a Nazirite, dedicated to God from the womb. He will take the lead in delivering Israel from the hands of the Philistines" (Judges 13:5 NIV). A person could become a Nazirite for a period of time by taking certain vows, including letting his hair grow. When "the hair of his consecration" (Numbers 6:19 ESV) was shaved off, it signaled the end of the vow and release from God's special service.

But Samson was called "from the womb" to be a Nazarite, blessed with great strength which led to outstanding victories and a fearful reputation for twenty years. Despite God's blessing, Samson had a mixed record. Alongside his successes, he chose a foreign wife, slept with a prostitute, beat and robbed men, and ultimately chose a lover from among Israel's enemies—who famously became his downfall.

Samson never learned the lesson Paul stressed: "Do not be misled: 'Bad company corrupts good character'" (1 Corinthians 15:33 NIV). He presumed on God's blessing, grew complacent, and ultimately chose this world over his calling. Though he repented in the end, his presumption cost him his life.

PRAY:

God my Father, humble me always to hold Your calling sacred so I am not deceived by my own success.

emotion possible. Joyful? Terrified? Hopeful? Angry? Confused? Thankful? You'll find it in Psalms.

Songs (and poetry) have always been a way to express the range of the human experience, putting feelings into words that resonate with the listener. King David was a prolific psalmist, but about half the book is authored by others—the Sons of Korah, Asaph, and even Moses.

Why is a song catalog *wisdom* literature? Because the wise man expresses himself honestly. He takes his complaints and troubles to a God who loves him since He is the source of hope and rescue. He trumpets his thanks and praise to the one who deserves adoration. And in being open about his own life, the psalmist teaches others to walk in wisdom, not to be influenced by the *wicked*, the *sinner*, or the *scoffer*. The Psalms confirm God's goodness, love, and sovereign wisdom without dismissing the hardships, sin, and injustice of this world.

PRAY:

I will sing of Your goodness, O God,
and confess what's on my heart to You.
You are my life and my hope.

MEDITATING

Read Psalm 119:9–16

KEY VERSES:

I rejoice in following your statutes as one
rejoices in great riches. I meditate on your
precepts and consider your ways. I delight in
your decrees; I will not neglect your word.
PSALM 119:14–16 NIV

CONTEMPLATE:

- What three words does the psalmist use to describe God's Word?

- What does the psalmist declare he will do with God's Word?

APPLY:

As believers, we are right to rejoice that we are "not under law, but under grace" (Romans 6:14 NIV). But being *under law* didn't mean the precepts and statutes of God were bad. On the contrary Paul said, "For we know that the law is spiritual, but I am of the flesh, sold under sin" (Romans 7:14 ESV). The problem lies with us, and the law's purpose was to make that clear. The longest psalm in the Bible is an acrostic poem (each section of eight lines begins with a letter of the Hebrew alphabet) that praises God for

SAUL'S FOLLY

Read 1 Samuel 15

KEY VERSE:

And Samuel said, "Has the LORD as great delight in burnt offerings and sacrifices, as in obeying the voice of the LORD? Behold, to obey is better than sacrifice, and to listen than the fat of rams.

1 SAMUEL 15:22 ESV

CONTEMPLATE:

- Why is obedience so important to the Lord?

- Is it possible to honor God but not obey Him?

APPLY:

Though God had created Israel as a unique people for Himself, after entering the Promised Land, they insisted on having a king to "be like all the nations" (1 Samuel 8:20 ESV). Samuel the prophet was rightly upset. But God said, "they have not rejected you, but they have rejected me from being king over them" (1 Samuel 8:7 ESV). So God gave them Saul, "as handsome a young man as could be found anywhere in Israel, and he was a head taller than anyone else" (1 Samuel 9:2 NIV).

But despite his early successes, Saul was not "a man after [God's] own heart" (1 Samuel 13:14 ESV).

Instead of destroying the Amalekites and their livestock per God's sovereign judgment, Saul allowed his men to take the best animals, and he himself enslaved their king as a trophy. When confronted, Saul excused his disobedience by saying that they took "the best of the things devoted to destruction, to sacrifice to the LORD your God in Gilgal" (1 Samuel 15:21 ESV). Saul actually tried to cover up his sin in the name of religious fervor! And his foolishness cost him everything: "Because you have rejected the word of the LORD, he has also rejected you from being king" (1 Samuel 15:23 ESV).

Solomon may have had Saul in mind when he said, "To draw near [to God] to listen is better than to offer the sacrifice of fools" (Ecclesiastes 5:1 ESV).

PRAY:

Almighty God, teach me to listen and humble me to obey without making excuses!

ENGAGING THE PSALMS

Read Psalm 1

KEY VERSES:

Blessed is the person who does not walk in the counsel of the wicked, nor stand in the path of sinners, nor sit in the seat of scoffers! But his delight is in the Law of the LORD, and on His Law he meditates day and night.

PSALM 1:1–2 NASB

CONTEMPLATE:

- What are the three things a person needs to avoid to be blessed?

- What does a wise person choose to focus on?

- What habit arises from delighting in God's Word?

APPLY:

Let's review some of the wisdom literature we've studied so far—Job, an epic poem about suffering and God's sovereignty; Proverbs, a collection of sayings of and about wisdom; and Ecclesiastes, a memoir of the meaninglessness of life apart from God. Now we'll look at the book of Psalms—literally a catalog of songs that cover virtually every human emotion possible. Joyful? Terrified? Hopeful? Angry? Confused? Thankful? You'll find it in Psalms.

Songs (and poetry) have always been a way to express the range of the human experience, putting feelings into words that resonate with the listener. King David was a prolific psalmist, but about half the book is authored by others—the Sons of Korah, Asaph, and even Moses.

Why is a song catalog *wisdom* literature? Because the wise man expresses himself honestly. He takes his complaints and troubles to a God who loves him since He is the source of hope and rescue. He trumpets his thanks and praise to the one who deserves adoration. And in being open about his own life, the psalmist teaches others to walk in wisdom, not to be influenced by the *wicked*, the *sinner*, or the *scoffer*. The Psalms confirm God's goodness, love, and sovereign wisdom without dismissing the hardships, sin, and injustice of this world.

PRAY:
I will sing of Your goodness, O God,
and confess what's on my heart to You.
You are my life and my hope.

MEDITATING

Read Psalm 119:9–16

KEY VERSES:

I rejoice in following your statutes as one rejoices in great riches. I meditate on your precepts and consider your ways. I delight in your decrees; I will not neglect your word.
PSALM 119:14–16 NIV

CONTEMPLATE:

- What three words does the psalmist use to describe God's Word?

- What does the psalmist declare he will do with God's Word?

APPLY:

As believers, we are right to rejoice that we are "not under law, but under grace" (Romans 6:14 NIV). But being *under law* didn't mean the precepts and statutes of God were bad. On the contrary Paul said, "For we know that the law is spiritual, but I am of the flesh, sold under sin" (Romans 7:14 ESV). The problem lies with us, and the law's purpose was to make that clear. The longest psalm in the Bible is an acrostic poem (each section of eight lines begins with a letter of the Hebrew alphabet) that praises God for

His *statutes*, *precepts*, and *decrees*.

As we've seen, the blessed man "meditates" on God's law day and night (Psalm 1:2). Deeper Bible study requires meditation—not the kind that empties the mind but the opposite. After Moses's death, God commanded Joshua, "Keep this Book of the Law always on your lips; *meditate on it day and night*, so that you may be careful to do everything written in it" (Joshua 1:8 NIV). Meditating means chewing on a verse or passage thoughtfully like you might savor a bite of steak. It means camping out on a passage for a while, perhaps committing it to memory. Maybe a proverb from this study keeps coming to mind, or the Spirit impresses you with something Paul wrote. Just like that steak, start with one bite at a time and see what God shows you as you chew on it.

PRAY:

*With the psalmist, I rejoice in the riches
of Your Word, O Lord my God!*

WILLING OBEDIENCE

Read Psalm 32

KEY VERSES:

I will instruct you and teach you in the way which you should go; I will advise you with My eye upon you. Do not be like the horse or like the mule, which have no understanding, whose trappings include bit and bridle to hold them in check, otherwise they will not come near to you.

PSALM 32:8–9 NASB

CONTEMPLATE:

- What promises does God make in this verse?

- What does He warn us about?

- What characterizes a horse or mule that might apply to us?

APPLY:

A student of scripture is only as wise as his willingness to take what he learns to heart. As we've seen, wisdom abides in the inner man which leads to right living because we are growing in our knowledge of God as we are "conformed to the image of His Son" (Romans 8:29 NASB). Sounds simple, right? But we all know from experience that we sometimes resist God.

The beginning of Psalm 32 points to one possible problem: unconfessed sin. We can't harbor known iniquity without creating conflict with a God who has a different plan for us: "When I kept silent, my bones wasted away. . . . Day and night your hand was heavy on me" (Psalm 32:3–4 NIV).

But what if there's truly nothing to confess? Perhaps there's a different heart issue. James instructed some believers to "purify your hearts, for your loyalty is divided between God and the world" (James 4:8 NLT). Growing in wisdom means we face choices—but we're not alone. God Himself is the one instructing us *with His eye upon us*—not to catch us in wrongdoing, but to strengthen us to draw near. We are to participate willingly, not require "bit and bridle" to pull us along like a horse or mule. What good would that be to us or our Father?

PRAY:

Patient Father, thank You for drawing me closer; teach me to cooperate!

THE DAYS WE ARE GRANTED

Read Psalm 90

KEY VERSE:
So teach us to number our days, that we may present to You a heart of wisdom.
PSALM 90:12 NASB

CONTEMPLATE:

- How many days have you already lived?

- How many more days do you hope to live?

- What is the goal of seeing ourselves as finite creatures?

APPLY:

Accounting for race, ethnicity, and lifestyle decisions, the average lifespan of an American male is about seventy-six years or 27,758 days. Psalm 90, the only psalm directly attributed to Moses, describes a similar average lifespan: "The years of our life are seventy, or even by reason of strength eighty; yet their span is but toil and trouble; they are soon gone, and we fly away" (Psalm 90:10 ESV).

Moses, who himself lived to 120, was making a pointed statement: no matter how long we live, compared to the Ancient of Days for whom a thousand years are "as yesterday when it is past, or as a watch in the night" (Psalm 90:4 ESV), our days are obviously limited.

James expressed a similar sentiment when he warned those who presumed upon the future saying, "you do not know what tomorrow will bring. What is your life? For you are a mist that appears for a little time and then vanishes" (James 4:14 ESV). James wasn't trying to be pessimistic about life just realistic, and he followed with this admonition: "Instead you ought to say, 'If the Lord wills, we will live and do this or that'" (James 4:15 ESV).

Moses and James both suggested the same perspective: the brevity of life gives us reason to choose carefully how we invest the days we've been granted, not just to gain a heart of wisdom for ourselves but when the time comes to present that heart as faithful stewards to the Creator.

PRAY:

Teach me to number my remaining days rightly, Father, that I may invest them in Your kingdom.

PERSONAL HISTORY

Read Psalm 107

KEY VERSES:

Give thanks to the LORD, for he is good! His faithful love endures forever. . . . Those who are wise will take all this to heart; they will see in our history the faithful love of the LORD.
PSALM 107:1,43 NLT

CONTEMPLATE:

- Thinking back over your history with God, what eventful moments stand out to you?

- Do you feel confident that you have a "story" to tell others about God's faithfulness?

APPLY:

Psalm 107 is a song about how God rescues His people over and over from all manner of troubles, with the repeated refrain: " 'Lord, help!' they cried in their trouble, and he rescued them from their distress" (Psalm 107:6,13,19,28 NLT). God's history with Israel as a nation illustrates how He deals with us as individuals, with enduring and faithful love.

God calls some men to become theologians or apologists to defend the faith in erudite ways and to "exalt [God] publicly before the congregation and before the leaders of the nation" (Psalm 107:32 NLT). That may apply to you, but *all believers* are called to testify to God's faithfulness in their own life. Your experience with Him is meant to be shared in a way that's real, providing a unique testimony that no one else has. "Has the LORD redeemed you? Then speak out! Tell others he has redeemed you from your enemies" (Psalm 107:2 NLT).

Even if you're young in the Lord, His history with you goes much further back than yours with Him! In fact, long before you were born: "Your eyes saw my unformed body; all the days ordained for me were written in your book before one of them came to be" (Psalm 139:16 NIV).

Think about the history of your life and consider documenting the things that celebrate God's faithfulness so you can share them with others.

PRAY:
You are good and loving to me, O God!
I proclaim Your faithfulness to the world!

LEGACY

Read Matthew 2:1–12

KEY VERSES:

Now after Jesus was born in Bethlehem of Judea in the days of Herod the king, behold, wise men from the east came to Jerusalem, saying, "Where is he who has been born king of the Jews? For we saw his star when it rose and have come to worship him."

MATTHEW 2:1–2 ESV

CONTEMPLATE:

- What were these wise men seeking?

- How did they know to look for this "king of the Jews"?

- What sign did they claim identified this new king?

APPLY:

Some Bible stories take a bit of "unlearning." Manger scenes often feature Jesus, His parents, some shepherds and animals. . .and three wise men. Feels good but it's inaccurate. The number *three* is an assumption based on the gifts presented (Matthew 2:11), and their arrival may have been a year or two *after* Jesus was born (Matthew 2:16).

The more traditional rendering of "magi from the east," however, is very accurate. This word traces its roots to the Persian Empire, which conquered the Babylonians where Daniel had been taken into captivity and distinguished himself. "[Daniel] was found to have insight and intelligence and wisdom like that of the gods. . . . King Nebuchadnezzar, appointed him chief of the magicians, enchanters, astrologers and diviners" (Daniel 5:11 NIV). "Then at Belshazzar's command, Daniel. . .was proclaimed the third highest ruler in the kingdom" (Daniel 5:29 NIV). "Daniel so distinguished himself among the administrators and the satraps by his exceptional qualities that the king [Darius] planned to set him over the whole kingdom" (Daniel 6:3 NIV).

The magi visited Jesus because of Daniel's legacy. His faithful testimony to a Divine King lasted hundreds of years, despite being in the extreme minority.

No one can ensure his own legacy, but God builds on faithfulness. A life of wisdom that points to Christ is the seed God uses in the lives that come after us.

PRAY:

Father, by Your Spirit, I want to remain faithful and allow You to use me as You see fit.

EXPECTING A KINGDOM

Read Matthew 5:1–12

KEY VERSES:

*And he opened his mouth and taught
them, saying: "Blessed are. . ."*
MATTHEW 5:2–3 ESV

CONTEMPLATE:

- What are the types of people that Jesus called "blessed" in Matthew 5?

- What are the promises He makes to each of these people?

APPLY:

Matthew 5–7 records the Sermon on the Mount (also called The Beatitudes)—Jesus' longest teaching in scripture. And it was so extraordinary that "when Jesus finished these sayings, the crowds were astonished at his teaching, for he was teaching them as one who had authority, and not as their scribes" (Matthew 7:28–29 ESV). Jesus' authority was evident because He spoke with wisdom from above, that is, from the perspective of the Kingdom of heaven. And that turned more than a few expectations upside down.

Matthew 5 begins with a series of proclamations for the types of people Jesus described as "blessed" (happy or to be envied)—if you were in one of these categories, you were fortunate "for/because" of the reasons that followed. Interestingly the first (the poor in spirit, Matthew 5:3) and last (those persecuted for righteousness' sake, Matthew 5:10) have identical reasons to be happy—"for theirs *is* the kingdom of heaven"—while the others are all promised *they shall* receive a corresponding reward. The list highlights the tension of the Kingdom for all believers: it exists between *already-have* and *will-inherit.*

The Promised Land provides a metaphor for the Kingdom. God commanded, "And you *shall take* possession of the land and settle in it, for I *have given* the land to you to possess it" (Numbers 33:53 ESV). Like those Israelites, we *have* and *will have* an inheritance from God. But if our expectations aren't based on both the present gift of the Kingdom *and* the future promise of heaven, then we will never walk in the fullness of wisdom.

PRAY:

Heavenly Father, teach me to walk in the reality of Your present and future Kingdom.

THE RETURN OF CHRIST

Read Luke 12:35–48

KEY VERSES:

Peter said, "Lord, are you telling this parable for us or for all?" And the Lord said, "Who then is the faithful and wise manager, whom his master will set over his household, to give them their portion of food at the proper time? Blessed is that servant whom his master will find so doing when he comes."

LUKE 12:41–43 ESV

CONTEMPLATE:

- What two qualities describe the kind of manager the Lord is talking about?
- What is the responsibility of the manager?

APPLY:

Scripture is filled with various styles of communication, from the poetic language of prophets to the matter-of-fact reporting in Judges. Even the Son of God had a distinct manner of speaking. Two of Jesus' patterns come together in today's passage—His use of metaphors and His habit of answering a question with a question.

Jesus shared several parables about being ready for His return. Sometimes He appears as a bridegroom, sometimes a nobleman, or as in today's passage, a master on a journey. In each case, the theme is always *Be wise! Don't be caught unaware!*

At first, Jesus appears to ignore Peter's question about whether the parable includes inside information or not. Instead of giving a straight answer, He pushed Peter to think. Did Peter see himself as a "faithful and wise manager" of what God had entrusted to him? Did he really want the responsibility? Because "from the one who has been entrusted with much, much more will be asked" (Luke 12:48 NIV). But being ready for Christ also comes with rewards: "[the master] will dress himself to serve, will have [the servants] recline at the table and will come and wait on them" (Luke 12:37 NIV). As with so much in scripture, there's a choice to be made. "Whoever has ears to hear, let them hear" (Luke 14:35 NIV).

PRAY:

Eternal Father, help me to live wisely and faithfully as I await the return of Jesus!

ABOUT THE AUTHOR

Jess MacCallum is the President of Professional Printers, Inc. in Columbia, South Carolina, where he has lived since graduating from the University of South Carolina in 1986. He has authored three books on marriage and family, and appeared twice on FamilyLife Today, with Dr. Dennis Rainey. He has also written hundreds of daily devotionals, including *The 30-Day Prayer Challenge for Men* published in 2019 (Barbour Publishing). His self-published novel, *The Chronicle of Delk the Uneven*, was released in 2021.

Jess also works as a leadership coach with two organizations, and manages his son's Celtic Folk Rock band, SYR. He has been married to Anne, a singer-songwriter and worship leader, for over 35 years. They have three grown children.